NON-FICTION

NON-FICTION

*UEA Postgraduate
Creative Writing Anthology
2018*

CONTENTS

D. J. TAYLOR
Foreword

When I first came across the phrase 'creative non-fiction' I assumed it was one of those expressions – like 'liberal Conservative' or 'stable Italian political system' – fated to collapse under the weight of its internal contradictions: a sound idea maybe, but procedurally impossible. Oddly, a few moments' thought confirmed that, all unknowing and many years ago, I was an early exponent of the genre myself.

It all happened back in the late 1980s when *The Spectator* announced that they intended to fund a prize for travel writing in memory of Shiva Naipaul, Sir Vidia's younger brother and, for my money, quite as adept a stylist as his distinguished elder sibling. If there was a drawback it lay in the fact that, taking my cue from Malcolm Muggeridge, who was once filmed in front of the Taj Mahal declaring that 'travel narrows the mind,' I had barely journeyed anywhere.

On the other hand, I was a serious fan of what might be called Hollywood travelogues. These were hard-boiled, hard-bitten accounts of hanging about in two-bit sleazy dives a couple of doors down from the Whiskey-a-Go-Go or the Viper Lounge, chewing the fat with regular guys who just might have had a walk-on in some low-rent horror movie back in 1965 and claimed to have witnessed, say, the late John Belushi, out of his head on fast white powders, tottering off the set of *Saturday Night Live*.

I could do this, I thought, and so I did. My first effort was a 3,000 word travel piece – the situational detail mostly filched from the essays collected by Martin Amis in *The Moronic Inferno* (1986), and *Wired* (1984), Bob Woodward's biography of Belushi – entitled 'On the Strip', as in Sunset. To my surprise, it came in as one of the runners-up (the overall winner might have been Hilary Mantel.) To my even greater surprise, a couple of years later, it was accepted for the Bloomsbury anthology *Soho Square*.

At the launch of this compendium, I shyly admitted my imposture to the editor, Ian Hamilton, who remarked that he'd thought some of the detail pretty authentic. Only Jonathan Coe, set to appraise the volume in the *London Review of Books,* wondered whether the piece's animating spirit might not have been pastiche rather than first-hand observation. But by this stage there was no stopping me. I wrote another piece, about a Christmas Day spent in a non-existent hotel, which appeared in the *Spec.*

I also continued with another little literary scheme, which was the writing of folksy short stories set in America – a country which I had not yet visited. These had titles like 'At Brackus's' and 'Saturday Night at the Jenks Motel.' A visiting US academic, to whom I guiltily owned up, told me not to worry. America was so weird these days, he explained, so socially fragmented and geographically disparate, that my imaginary take was just as valid as Garrison Keillor's.

And so I scribbled on about the lives of those old-timers in Cook County, Tennessee, or the view from Nowhere, Nebraska. Back then I assumed that I was infringing an elemental literary law and that sooner or later some custodian of the eternal verities would make me pay. Now I realise that, like the contributors to this sparkling anthology, I was simply being creative. Unlike them, on the other hand, I was merely making it up. Gathering up the broken shards of lived experience is a whole lot harder than those exercises in sleight of hand and I congratulate all these present for the reimagined versions of real life they have so dextrously brought to the printed page.

KATHRYN HUGHES
Introduction

Our non-fiction writers this year have spread their wings to take on an extraordinary range of subjects, places and, indeed, genres. With Aaron Deary we travel to Bardsey Island, a spot of land off the Welsh coast buried in deep time. It's here that the Bardsey Apple, mythological and material grandparent to the sweetest crunchiest apples in the world, has its roots. From there it's off to India in the 1990s to watch Saloni Prasad go through the laceratingly painful and brilliantly funny business of failing to master Kathak, a form of classical dance which is meant to be graceful. In Saloni's hands – and feet – it becomes a ritual humiliation.

Failing minds and memories are everywhere. Romana Canneti brings her lawyer's sensibility to the muddled present and spectacularly faceted past of Manuela Sykes, an elderly Alzheimer's patient who turns out to have lived a life of rackety glamour and tireless political engagement. Fugitive, too, are the memories of Ingrid Fagundez's grandmother, who struggles to understand what is going on but knows the importance of always staying cheerful. It is only by delving into her grandparents' courtship letters from the 1950s that Ingrid, a Brazilian journalist, starts to understand why that equanimity might be so hard won.

The magnificently-named Justus Flair gives us a revealing account of what it's like to be 'an endling,' one of the last people on earth (as far as she knows) to bear her surname. As for her first name – just don't spell it 'Justice,' no matter how noble it might sound. The importance of names and identities comes to the fore also for Freya Dean, who delivers a tense and subtle account of what it feels like to be caught up in the clammy grip of sexual jealousy. Peiyi Li, meanwhile, delivers a wonderfully funny, brilliantly barbed account of cross-cultural love and hideous misunderstanding.

Cultural investigation is also the subject of Peter Goulding's bracing account of climbing slate in North Wales. It turns out that becoming a 'slatehead' means delving not only into intimate family histories but also excavating a larger story about political and social dissent in late 20th-century Britain. Place is equally vital and equally complex in Yin F Lim's mouth-watering account of what food means to the expatriate Malaysian community in Britain. Lorna Daymond, meanwhile, explains why, for her,

Thetford is brown and Bournemouth begins as blue but tails off to grey. It's called synaesthesia and it sounds like heaven.

Jess Morgan, a professional singer-songwriter, leaves her guitar behind and instead uses words to give a tender account of what going back to your hometown (Great Yarmouth in her case) feels like after you've spent so long on the road. Aaron O'Farrell, meanwhile, narrates a terrifying account of a high-speed police chase on the bumpy roads of Togo, West Africa, complete with a tractor blocking the way and pirated gasoline in the boot.

Sureshkumar Pasupula Sekar gives us a brilliantly vibrant account of what the score of *Titanic* meant to him as a child growing up in rural India. Meanwhile, Ivan Pope embarks on a bicycle ride through Europe, following the route which so many men, women and children were forced to take towards Auschwitz 80 years ago.

Kate Romain provides a wonderfully anarchic account of her imaginary conversations with the scribbling stranger sitting opposite her in a cramped mid-winter café. Susan Woolliams goes on the trail of two remarkable women – Emma Paolozzi, daughter and caretaker of her esteemed artist father Eduardo, and Sister Christa, the German nun who moved through the world like a Dalek but cared about it profoundly all the same.

This diverse anthology comprises the latest work from the 2018 cohort of non-fiction writers studying UEA's renowned Creative Writing MA.

Romana Canneti became a barrister by way of an earlier career as a television producer. She specialises in media law. Her writing has appeared in *The Guardian*, *The Independent* and the *British Review of Journalism*. She lives in London and is working on a book about Manuela Sykes.

Manuela

It was her profile: the beaky nose and jutting chin, the lips pintucked like hospital sheets over naked gums. Manuela's face, says my notebook entry from the day we met in December 2016, recalls a raptor. Shamefully, I hadn't noticed the dearth of teeth before fetching a slice of millionaire's shortbread from the cake counter. Her friend Roger patiently chopped layers of caramel, chocolate and biscuit into tiny bites so Manuela could work each morsel around her mouth before swallowing.

The sugary treat over, the large dark-blue eyes, red-rimmed and hooded, fixed on me again. Their purple sockets betrayed the strain of her animal alertness, the terror evoked by dementia's magpie thieving: a permanent stasis of fight or flight, a non-stop feed of cortisol.

Why am I here? Who are these people? Take me home to Mummy.

Perhaps, it struck me, the watchful stare was muscle memory – Manuela's face set in a grim parody of a self she could no longer assemble: politician, councillor, social activist, publisher. A woman who took no prisoners, who brooked no opposition. A trouble-maker, if you liked the status quo; a revolutionary, if you didn't.

But that day in the crypt-café of St Martins-in-the-Fields, she was fluffy as a baby goshawk. Someone – presumably a carer – had enveloped her slight frame in a shaggy pink coat, of the kind Anita Pallenberg might have worn on a stroll down the Portobello Road, hanging from Keith Richards's arm.

I had previously seen photos of Manuela: as a beaming teenager in school skirt and blazer; soft around the edges in her WREN uniform; out canvassing in a tailored tweed jacket with nipped-in waist, a spotted silk foulard around her neck. Manifestly a woman who loved clothes, who cared to look elegant. I couldn't imagine she'd have gone for a furry pastel coat, given the choice, although there was some evidence of recent grooming: her nails were dyed a scuffed scarlet, her thinning hair a patchy brown. Feathery tufts stood proud of collar-length wisps.

Roger had instructed me to clap during the introductions. The old lady rewarded me with a smile of unexpected sweetness. Later, wordlessly sipping her tea, she punctuated our conversation with loud applause if women's rights, animals or her mother were mentioned. We received winks, frowns or dismissive sideways waves of her hand if they were not.

Roger tried to draw her in, to kindle a memory. 'D'you remember how you made the Queen pay rates, Manuela? In your days at Westminster Council?'

Manuela presented her profile, lips clamped. 'Men just squirt. Mummy is the only good one.'

Her companion smiled at the insult, gently stroked her hand, and tried again. 'How many times did you stand for Parliament Manuela? Wasn't it seven altogether?'

The clink of knives and crockery filled the silence.

When I got up to leave, I proffered my hand. Manuela took it, and grasped it firmly, not letting go for what felt like minutes. Her steel-cold grip was so strong that I thought, absurdly, she might break my bones. Her gaze did not waver as she squeezed harder and I felt an irrational spasm of guilt: I may look ridiculous, her eyes told me, but make no mistake: I know your game.

What *was* my game? I wasn't sure.

'She... wanted her life to go out with a bang, not a whimper,' wrote judge Anselm Eldergill.

It was 2014 and I, as a newspaper lawyer, had come across his judgement.[1] It was my introduction to the name Manuela Sykes. Manuela, I saw, had been fighting Westminster, the council she had once represented, to be released from a care home back to her flat in Pimlico.

---

1 www.bailii.org/ew/cases/EWHC/COP/2014/B9.html

Judges in the court of protection hear daily stories from the husks of human lives: those of people who lack the 'mental capacity' to decide how and where to live. But their rulings, then, were infrequently published.

'She has had a dramatic life,' I read of Manuela, 'and the drama is not yet over.'

Eldergill and I sheltered from the rain – a chance meeting under a carapace of scaffolding in Southampton Row – as I mentioned that I'd recently read his decision.

'She kept her windows permanently open for the pigeons to fly in; their droppings were everywhere. She is a remarkable woman you know. Such a sad case.' His admiration for the woman who'd appeared before him was patent.

Her short-term memory span had meant she couldn't understand her predicament, despite the capable-looking tweed suit and red lipstick. 'God knows why I've been plonked in this comfy prison,' she'd told the court, only minutes after receiving an explanation. 'If I'm not allowed home, I intend to slit my wrists.'

Then aged eighty-nine, Manuela had advanced dementia. Prone to nocturnal wanderings and dangerously underweight, she'd attacked a carer with her stick and had been sectioned. Nurses had been visiting in pairs 'for fear of their personal safety.'

Eldergill knew that Manuela had made a living will, in which she'd stipulated that quality of life should take precedence over quantity. She had never been risk averse. He ordered enhanced supervision arrangements and agreed to her trial return home.

Manuela's case, at first sight one of many involving the welfare of dementia sufferers, acquired a characteristically unique legal twist; one that chimed with my own campaign for journalists to be allowed into (previously closed) court of protection hearings. She had run a newspaper and stood for Parliament: accountability was her thing, too. In lifting the mandatory anonymity provisions at her request, Eldergill made his a landmark judgement. This final battle, like her others, was to be fought in the public eye.

Although Manuela had rallied the scattered fragments of a brilliant mind in court, it was a fleeting triumph. Just three weeks after her return to Pimlico, she fractured a new carer's rib and was back in the detested care home.

The story lodged like a pebble in my shoe. Was someone of such spirit – such *bravery* – to disappear like water in sand? What is a life; where does it go? Who was Manuela?

—

I tracked down the reporter who had covered the court case and he put me in touch with Manuela's niece. Over coffee near her office in Peckham Rye, Honey explained that as a social worker, she had opposed Manuela's wish to return home, convinced it could not be in her aunt's best interests. Honey knew little about Manuela's private life but was clearly proud that she had once been a formidable public figure. Shortly after we met, Honey emailed me a photo of a cartoon by Giles, the celebrated *Express* satirist, depicting a doughty Manuela contesting the 1958 Ipswich by-election.

Manuela's mother, Honey told me, had been Baroness Ottilie Von Hundelshausen, born of a German-Dutch lineage stretching back to the twelfth century. She had travelled to America where she met Manuela's father, a Yorkshireman who had joined the Canadian Mounties. The couple settled in Mexico where Manuela was born in 1925. Some years later they moved from Guadalajara to London, where the marriage foundered after the birth of Manuela's brother Darrell. The problem – probably the catalyst for Manuela's lifelong feminism – was Mr Sykes Snr's compulsive womanising.

Honey sketched childhood impressions of her aunt Manuela, a remote figure that she'd see only once a year on Halloween, which happened to be Ottilie's birthday.

For Honey and her sister Melody, the visits to the maisonette in Pimlico with their father ('a troubled man'), were tinged with glamour. Ottilie, resplendent in peacock-feathered Liberty-print silk gowns, would be presented with intricate miniature tableaux that an adoring Manuela had sculpted in her honour: marzipan Halloween figurines, painstakingly fashioned and hand-painted, the witches' hats and ghosts making an enchanting, somewhat odd, birthday cake. The high-ceilinged room with its dark, heavy German oak furniture, family heirlooms from grander days, curlicued with the Von Hundelshausen coat of arms; the imposing marble fireplace; a chimney breast hung with Chinoiscric wallpaper, its delicate tracery of birds and trees an exotic backdrop: it all seemed, to Honey's childish eyes, like a stage set. Pet poodles nestled with Manuela at her mother's feet.

Manuela kept her pledge never to put Ottilie, who suffered from dementia, in a home. But in 2006 she faced her own diagnosis of Alzheimer's disease alone. She had never married, had no children from whom to extract such a promise, and had lived alone since her mother's death in 1987.

Honey suggested I meet Roger, who had run the pioneering social care unit at St Martins that Manuela had helped set up, decades earlier, in 1948. As her disease took hold and concerns were raised at church about Manuela's increasingly dishevelled appearance, Roger had, Honey explained, kept a promise to his late wife to look after her friend Manuela. Since 2006 he'd visited Manuela five times a week, taking her on outings to church, to the cinema, to tea. He was at Manuela's side during her legal battle; his evidence had helped persuade the judge to sanction her short-lived return home.

—

Weeks after our tea at St Martins, Manuela's maisonette was sold to pay for her care.

'She doesn't know,' said Roger, his eyes filming with moisture. Manuela had deteriorated considerably, he added; he was no longer allowed to take her out. If I wanted to see her again it would have to be at the hospice.

There I saw Manuela's fellow inmates; captives, likewise, of the most pitiless of grim reapers. Not the skeletal one who leads us to the shores of death, but his cousin, the mind-reaper, who keeps his victims alive, locked in closed cells of mute suffering, unable to understand what has happened to them, to reassure those who love them that they are still present. The reaper's scythe shreds their psyches, leaving only physical husks, blunted stubs to be fed, washed, lifted from bed to chair. I despaired, now, of discovering much more about Manuela. She was dissolving into silence.

That day, I fed her. No longer a raptor, she opened her mouth like a little bird and sucked spoonfuls of puréed vegetables.

Back in Pimlico, while Manuela's flat was being emptied, I had glimpsed Roger's tall frame slumped in a chair, features fleetingly awry like a cubist portrait, the customary mask of gentlemanly humour set aside. It was an icy March afternoon: there was no heating or electricity, so our curfew was dusk. Her nieces had removed family heirlooms, but the maisonette's grubby floor was scattered with items they'd left behind. Exhausting though it was, Roger laboured to salvage the person Manuela had been, transporting her possessions in his little turquoise Peugeot. Just her printing press defeated him. He was taking them, he told me, to his garden shed – for me to sift through and order into an account of her life. Gratitude was the only polite reaction.

I think they come flat-packed in Homebase. The shed in New Malden stood roughly halfway down Roger's garden. Past a clump of cheery tangerine-coloured poppies, I picked my way down a path of stepping stones across a haphazardly mown lawn. The long, narrow garden was enclosed on both sides by tall, orangey-wood fencing; the ginger theme picked up by the russet of the shed's rough timbers. The vaguely Alpine pitched roof was ornamented, Heidi-style, by a wavy gable trim above the door.

Inside, a four-paned window let in diagonal sunbeams that ribboned the penumbra. They illuminated Manuela's books and records; her filing cabinets crammed with cuttings and letters from associates – Lord Soper, Jeremy Thorpe, Tony Benn; boxed campaign leaflets for the homeless, women, and animals; folders with anti-apartheid flyers; Liberal and Labour election manifestos; Common-Ownership Movement treatises; her leader columns for her newspaper *The Voice of the Unions*; Free Palestine banners; Manuela's walnut writing desk; her chair.

The shed was the repository of a life's work, a symbol of immortality and the intended workplace for Manuela Sykes's prospective biographer: me. It was her Taj Mahal. Hers was a story, I understood that afternoon, that I would tell.

Roger passed Manuela's final nights in a chair by her hospital bed. He told me, after she died, something I already knew.

'I think, now, that I was in love with Manuela'.

Lorna Daymond has gained a steady flow of life experiences and has previously written short stories and a play for BBC Radio 4. After attending a teacher training college in Canterbury, studying English and listening to The Beatles, Lorna taught primary school-aged children before leading Norfolk's Gypsy and Traveller Education Service for over twenty years.

Union of the Senses

I've grown used to people looking at me strangely if I say that the word 'Thetford' is brown, that 'Bournemouth' begins blue but tails off to grey and brown, whereas 'Wymondham Station' is green, brown, yellow and vermilion. Until ten years ago, I assumed it had something to do with the way I must have been taught to read and write, possibly using a word and picture for each letter of the alphabet; it seemed a logical explanation. Perceiving letters, and digits, in particular colours didn't bother me. In fact it was helpful, so I wondered about it only occasionally; until I realised that other people's brains don't seem to work like mine. Let me explain, because you may see things quite differently.

In my mind, the letter S, maybe at one time linked to the image of a sun, is bright yellow even when it's printed in black. G is green, possibly associated with a blob of green or the picture of grass or a gate? B or b is blue; no mental picture here except perhaps a blob of blue. D, W, F are also green. Fish? Water? I have no idea why D is green, it just is. The letter R (could the picture have been a rose? Or a splash of red paint?) is red. Not any old red though. Never vermilion. A is carmen red with a hint of orange, C is pale cream, H and T are brown, different browns. N is dark blue, almost navy. Y is mid-grey. The whole alphabet is a rainbow.

I am told that seeing letters or words as colours, even if they are printed or written in black, is an indication of synaesthesia; a lovely word, with or without the central *ae*. People may know that 'anaesthesia' means having no sensation. 'Synaesthesia' or syn*ae*sthesia means joined sensation. Some people have joined sensations of taste or smell with everyday sounds such as doors opening or a car engine revving. Other people with synaesthesia see colours when they hear particular musical notes being played.

Not much is known about how synaesthesia develops, but it has been suggested that this starts in early childhood. Nothing to do with reading schemes as such. It would appear to develop when children are intensively engaged for the first time with abstract concepts. That hypothesis would explain why the most common forms of synaesthesia are grapheme-colour, spatial sequence and number form. These are usually the first abstract concepts that educational systems, families and everyday life require children to learn.

I remember my postcode not only by the NATO alphabet for reciting over the telephone but because I see it picked out in white on a street sign. For me, it's navy blue, red, grey, terracotta followed by 9 (dark blue, not navy, there's a difference) B (mid-blue) G (green). The next street is called Green Lane. My mental picture is green, red, brown, brown, dark blue; then a different blue, red-orange, dark blue, brown.

And to make life more confusing for others but simpler for me, I also have spatial sequence synaesthesia so I see numbers or numerical sequences as points in space. I discovered that only when I asked someone where her 100 was.

And I have a mental three-dimensional map of numbers, days of the week and months of the year, which runs anti-clockwise. I find it most helpful, better than a diary or calendar. My mental map of the year is punctuated by slight gaps where school holidays would have occurred, so I guess the theory about synaesthesia forming when abstract concepts such as 'term-time' and 'weekend' also develop, has some merit.

I am stuck for a verb here. I'm not sure whether I *have* synaesthesia; I certainly don't *suffer* from it because it's very helpful in remembering things. So I guess synaesthesia is a condition which I *enjoy*. And although I might wish to explain myself as being synaesthetic, it makes me sound as if I am either man-made or not real: or sin aesthetic, engaged in the production of very beautiful but pornographic films. Which, as yet, I am not.

Freya Dean was born in the Netherlands and lives in Cambridge. Her work pays attention to time and place but moves always towards interior questions of intimacy, self-knowledge and love. On the MA programme at UEA she has completed a novel-length memoir and is currently working on a collection of short pieces that combine the tenets of prose, essay and poetry.

Fault Lines

It was later that day – after Alma came upstairs to warn me to close the windows and before the rain arrived – that I found the book.

I was searching for a postcard from my grandfather; a reproduction of M C Escher's *Belvedere*, its figures cloaked and hooded, the building an elegant impossibility. I thought I could write about Escher as a way of writing about my grandfather. The idea had come from a Brown community class, 'Poetry & Voice', that I'd taken the semester just gone. The class had been *a way of keeping you out of trouble* – Tom's words. He didn't say them with condescension, though at the time I'd reacted furiously. I couldn't see it, but my husband understood more than anyone how unsuited I was to playing a young campus wife, moving through the rooms of our East Side apartment as if I might find within them the sense of purpose I'd left in London.

It was my habit to tuck correspondence inside books, for safekeeping, and so I worked through the shelves in the front room, taking each volume out and unsettling its pages. I did not find the card and moved on to the bookcases in the study.

Wind was glancing the leaves of a silver birch against the window and the sky through the glass appeared yellow; thick with gathering cloud. It was possible to hear heavy traffic on the streets below – cars and trucks moving south down Gano to join the interstate and west, towards Providence. Still the room seemed quiet and apart: Tom's domain.

There were papers on the floor and on the desk. A tea-stained mug topped one pile and for a moment I considered returning it to the kitchen. Then I sat down before three low bookcases that spanned the wall beneath the window and looked through a row of large hardbacks. Their titles meant nothing to me: *Measure Theory, Large Deviations, Stochastic Differential Equations*. I replaced each one with care – though really it was not care, but a kind of distrust. These books belonged to a dimension of my husband's life that I could not enter or even approach and although our marriage was still new, that summer I had begun to see how this difference would always hold a part of him away.

15

As I started on the next shelf, I noticed a book at odds with the rest. It was slim, with a cream dust jacket that puckered slightly. *THE PROPHET/ KAHLIL GIBRAN* was printed in bold Gothic type along the spine. I had never seen this book and took it out, immediately startled by the cover. It resembled nothing Tom would read.

I turned the book over, back again, opened it – and a photograph fell out. It slipped to the floor with as little significance as if a stranger had brushed past me in the street. The picture was of Tom, and a woman. They were standing on top of a building, red-tiled rooftops forming a stepped horizon behind them. Her body was leaning into his body and his left arm sloped easily around her back. My husband's other arm was outstretched, supporting the camera which had taken the photograph.

This woman was many things that I at once registered I was not, as if her presence even in that static image were able to announce an absence, or deficit, in myself. She wore cut off shorts and a black halterneck top which laid bare tanned shoulders and legs and together communicated a bold confidence in her body. A pair of sunglasses had been pushed up onto her head, holding back hair that was long and blonde. Sun was causing both her and Tom to squint. They looked happy. Light, joyful. I recognised it: one of them, at least, was in love with the other.

I sat on the floor. As if someone might see me – though I knew Tom would be at work for many hours yet – I slipped the photo back between the pages of the book. I didn't want to look at it, but with equal force I did. Instead I looked with effort at *The Prophet* itself.

Chapters included 'Love', 'Marriage' and 'Children'. The narrative was first person verse with an instructive, self-possessed tone that fell somewhere between scripture and poetry. Many passages opened with a command: 'Love one another', 'Give your hearts'. I was surprised to recognise a few phrases: 'Let there be spaces in your togetherness', 'Make not a bond of love'; and resented that I had done. Interleaved with the text were full-page illustration plates depicting men and women coupled, or in small groups. All of them were naked, their bodies pressed together and eyes closed in a gesture that could have been deference or rapture.

As I worked through the book's pages I began to understand the degree of intimacy that weighed behind its gift. It was, also, a lovely thing. A beautifully made hardback edition, with stitched binding and hand cut paper, published by a small American imprint.

I took the photograph out and turned it over. On the reverse was an inscription: *To Tom, with Love, Nicole.* I noted with disgust that she had drawn a smiley face beside her name, though the face overleaf did not look especially young – nor was Tom's; this was not an age ago, but the very recent past. I felt this, but I couldn't know it, until visible in the corner of the frame was Tom's Karrimor backpack. I'd been with him the day he'd bought it, the spring before the summer that he'd left to travel Europe – and at the end of which trip our own relationship had begun.

—

I knew of only one serious relationship of Tom's. A girl called Erin, whom he'd met during his last year of university in a bar on Birmingham's Victoria Square, each of them home for the winter break. I was certain she was not the woman in the photograph; the chronology did not fit.

Erin and Tom were together for the remainder of his time at Cambridge, but I had left the city by then and it was easy for me to pretend none of this was happening. Tom never mentioned her. It was other friends who did, and when they spoke it was important to me to forget every detail of what had been said – whether they seemed in favour of her, whether she was studying in London or had now graduated; even whether she existed at all.

And yet this woman continued to pass through my life as a ghost might, when I least expected it and even after circumstances had changed.

One evening Tom and I were sitting in the front room of a Georgian house in Islington. He had recently started work in London, where I was into my second job at *ELLE*. The Georgian terrace was Tom's new accommodation – a Peabody Trust houseshare that some welfare connection of his mother's had enabled. It was the clumsy, awkward week when our friendship had accelerated into something that was not yet defined and upon which so much rested that it was hard to risk stealing even a glance at it. I cared for Tom furiously, had done so for too long against a backdrop of going out with other people who mattered nothing to me, first in Cambridge, now in London. Then he'd asked me outright, at the Seven Dials crossroads in Covent Garden – *don't you think it's us who should go out together?* But it was no longer that simple; we'd been doing that, under cover, for years.

Tom and I ate around a small table in the front room, bay window overlooking the North London street. August. Dusk arrived late. The chords of a guitar leaked through the wall of a house next door, a large fern draped from a corner, the sofa was a faded red and the scent of cigarettes was woven into its fabric. There was a salad he had made with raw fennel, slicing it thinly. I had never eaten it like this before and drew attention to it, pronouncing upon it – always trying a little to put him off, to see how far I could push this man. But in my mind this night became marked as the point of no return – the point at which I was in love with Tom and it was no longer possible to go back, or to remain unchanged if I tried.

Into the evening the phone rang. It had been quiet in the room and then this shrill noise. Tom answered it. He looked suddenly awkward; he wasn't expecting the call or it wasn't welcome. The conversation drifted to CDs, borrowed or lent, and arrangements for their return. Despite Tom's body language the call was friendly and went on a little. When he hung up the receiver I asked who it had been.

Just a friend, he said.

I thought how stupid, that he would think I of all people might believe this. Then I saw that he had said it with the understanding that it was a code, to spare both him and me an elaboration of this particular history. I decided it must be Erin, who I'd made such an effort to deny and who now appeared like a torn seam right through the middle of that evening. For a long time afterwards I wondered what he had liked about her, whether he had loved her, if I would consider her pretty, what brought them together and what had caused them to part. I tried not to think of them in bed together and tried also to forget how he had looked when speaking to her on the phone. I did not give voice to these questions, but they changed what existed between Tom and me. I was forced to see him as someone that others might want. It was no longer possible for me to pretend that he would wait forever for me to decide that it was him, and not someone else, who I wanted.

—

I made no mention of my discovery. Instead I fell into an ill temper, withdrew from any effort at conversation, all interest in sex. I saw that Tom took this as an expression of my increasing discontent with life in Providence – which only served to worsen my mood. I seized upon every small thing. If my husband went to wash up the plates from our supper I would take them from him and insist that I do it, crashing dishes against one another in the sink and allowing the tap to run wastefully. If Tom followed me to bed, putting away papers I knew he'd have read late into the night, I ignored him and turned to face the wall.

Late June and our first wedding anniversary loomed. Perhaps Tom saw this as an entrance – one evening he sat down beside the bath, took from me the magazine that I was reading, folded it and placed it in his lap.

Are you going to tell me what's wrong? he asked, touching lightly at my hair.

Nothing I said, and my husband retracted his hand; but he did not move.

What's wrong? he asked again.

I sat up in the water which had in any case lost its heat and I looked at him. The air in the room was soft, slack with humidity and the late hour and I thought how it was not the right time to do this, that night was settling over the apartment and the street outside and how once I had spoken everything would be altered. But the idea of this also pleased me.

Was your girlfriend, Erin, blonde?

Tom's answer arrived slowly: *No.*

Then who's the woman with you in the photograph, inside that book?

Aaron Deary worked as an English teacher in schools in London and Boston, Massachusetts. His writing explores the intersection between people and place. Currently, he is assembling a collage of non-fiction stories about the Irish Sea: tales from a different side of the British Isles.

Bardsey Island
(An extract)

—

'It is remarkable how closely the history of the apple tree is connected with that of man'' wrote Henry David Thoreau. A wild apple tree begins as a delicate spire amid a tangled brush of apple tree shoots. This sprawl was once a single sapling, vulnerable to the teeth and claws of casual predators. But for every shoot eaten, two more grew in its place. Over time, this cycle of damage and regeneration established a dense thicket of thorned branches that fenced the central growth from browsing animals. From this centre, inevitably, shoots strive upwards and one eventually reaches maturity. As this shoot grows, its spreading limbs shade its fortifications and its thicker roots drain the soil bed to feed the hungry trunk. The scrub that sacrificially facilitated the tree's growth will be betrayed. Shadowed from the sun and starved of the soil, the bush will shrivel and die. The tree will flourish.

—

1 Thoreau, H. (1862) 'Wild Apples', *The Atlantic*. [Online] Available at: www.theatlantic. com/magazine/archive/1862/11/wild-apples/411517/. (Accessed: 5th November 2017).

Across Wales, a rare type of apple tree grows. Its fruit is attractively flushed and exudes a citrusy perfume. But all trees that bear this fruit, bear also a hideous scar. This scar is caused by 'grafting'. This process involves connecting the roots and trunk of one type of apple tree to the branch network of another. These Frankenstein trees enable farmers to combine strengths: high yield branches are grown on gale-resistant roots. They are fused mid-trunk. For the apple with the citrus smell, every tree they fall from is thus scarred. Except one tree, the last tree of its kind. The fruit of this tree is the most fragrant, its shape the most distinct because its fruit and its roots are whole. This tree grows alone on a stormswept Welsh island called Bardsey Island. This tree survived by the gentle hands of monks; later, by the furtive grip of pirates, the heavy grasp of kings, maybe once by the bony reach of a wizard and eventually by the inquisitive grope of science. Photographs showed me this tree, sheltered in a recess of a high stone wall, neighboured by farmland and surrounded by the thunder of the Irish Sea.

From the Llyn peninsula in west Wales, nearby Bardsey Island resembles a monstrous snail, with a reaching head, striving to the south and a great bulge of land in the north. Beyond the western horizon of tufted wave-heads, Ireland waits. Geologists attribute the island's existence and shape to a colossal, undersea landslide. These distant events formed this tiny, spilt-drop of land that is home to fewer than ten people. It was not always so sparse. History records stable populations on the island as high as 120 permanent residents. But even that number does not account for the bones of 20,000 people rumoured to be buried in the one square mile of land. I travelled there to find the lonely apple tree and to see a land of bones, ruins and legend.

The journey to Bardsey Island is an unusual transition. Viewed from the deck of a boat, the island is lost in the scale of the sea. It is dark, its shape indistinct and it appears lifeless. It is a curious experience to approach an island with only the passing sea to offer perspective. Subtly and gently it swells in size. This quiet growth happens in contrast to the rushing wind and the bouncing boat. There is a disconnection between the journey and the destination. Movement seems fast; the approach seems slow. Eventually, the dark mass deepens into cliff flutes and grass banks; fractures and colours appear on the rocks. All the time, Bardsey Island comes to dominate the horizon more and more. Then the lump blinks with life. White dots appear and multiply, grow yellow beaks and stare back. Rounding the headland into a small bay, the ferry stirs life around the coast. Choughs – crows with blood-red legs and beaks – take off from the shore. Circling overhead, their cries ring but soon they settle. Beneath the surface of the water, grey skulls with hollow eyes stare unblinkingly upwards. Seals.

On land, when the boat engine cuts, noise is replaced by sound. Wind brushes gorse and the sea slops against rock. Stonechats click. All light is natural, the land is cast in sunshine or shadow. Rusty ferns coat the hillside and acres of pastureland glow green. Without vehicles and crowds, the stillness is deep. From any point, the rest of the island can be seen. To the south, a narrow peninsula stretches out and hosts a lighthouse; the west of the land is flat and portioned into grazing fields by dry stone walls. This patchwork of farmland dominates the space on the island. The large hill rises from the east coast and is the only notable topographical feature. At the foot of this hill, beside the grazing fields, the houses of the island gather. The infrastructure is modest. Some houses are white, most are grey. A wide track joins the houses. There are no roads; paths around the island have been trodden into place by habit. I was told by the ferryman that I can walk anywhere, so long as I remember to close gates behind me. Leaving the bay, I see some solitary trees and plot my wander until I find the mother tree of the Bardsey Apple.

I am walking on graves. In the sixth century, an age that prized scarcity and resilience, this remote island struck Saint Cadfan as the perfect setting for his monastery. The proximity to the mainland reveals nothing of its isolation. The quality, not the quantity of the sea demands reckoning. With its stealthy currents and stinging waves, this modest stretch of sea can still render the island unreachable. For Saint Cadfan in his medieval craft, the crossing was perilous. This peril, however, would soon prove the island's making as Cadfan's monastery grew in reputation and established itself as one of the most prominent pilgrimage sites in Northern Europe. The faithful knew that the island held the power of immortality: those who died and were buried here were promised the everlasting grace of heaven. 20,000 pilgrims, it is said, have been trusted to its sacred earth. Every building currently standing on the island disinterred bones when their foundations were laid. I was told to keep a look out for remains because many visitors have unearthed the grimace of so many unknown Yoricks.

Heading north, the hill on my right, a 'lowland' of pastures is before me. Isolated twitches of activity can be seen. Far ahead a dark figure is occupied by a fence post, probably mending wire. At the coast, someone is looking into the sky with binoculars. With four permanent residents, a handful of summer regulars and a steady trickle of tourists, the island is never empty. But it calls to the lonesome. I can see five people, but all are individual, hundreds of metres separate the closest two and their actions are all silent to me. The island's reputation for isolation and immortality can be traced so far back that it blurs into mythology.

Local lore insists that Bardsey Island's loneliest inhabitant is the wizard Merlin. It is said he was betrayed by his apprentice, Niviane. Her beauty confounded Merlin and he agreed to school her in his art and reveal to her the secrets of his staff. One night, as he slept, Niviane wove one of these spells over Merlin, trapping him in his slumber. Fearing his vengeance, she then took him to this remote island where it is said he is entombed somewhere, locked in a glass cage of Niviane's conjuring. He never woke. He waits, dormant but undying.

Walking on, I pass through paddocks with sheep grazing. Wind-stunted trees lean heavily to one side, their leafy heads distorted by buffeting gusts. Most trees on the island share this eerie, misshapen bend. They bow to the hill which shields the trees from contesting, correcting winds. Choughs land around me on tree branches and fence posts. They are large crows with a spindly, curved beak. I pause to watch them and before long am joined by a volunteer who has spent seven months here recording bird populations. 'Choughs are rare in the UK but common here and in Cornwall,' he tells me. On the fencepost, one chough dips into a deep, performative bow, its beak pointing backwards between its legs. It is their most distinguishing behaviour. I ask him why they do it. 'Depends who you ask,' he tells me 'I think it's to communicate with their mate. They pair for life. Each pair has a subtly different bow.' He pauses. 'Ask a farmer here, though, they say it's a bow of respect. To Merlin.' He marks a count of five choughs in his notebook and walks on, the chough continues to hold its bow.

There are three small copses on the island. All knotted willow trees. All pollarded. Their thick, squat trunks and long spindly withies are bare. It is early in the year for them to have lost their skirting leaves but Bardsey Island was blasted twice by the ferocious storms of late summer and life here has aged ahead of its season. Each copse belongs to a house to provide materials for lobster traps, basketry and thatching. The copse is dense, and in its centre the shadow is deep. Entering it, a phalanx of trunks obscures the surrounding green and branches hash the sky. After a few steps, light from the far side of the copse glimmers and the salt air again replaces the smell from the trees. The village of Nant can now be seen, maybe a half mile ahead. It is the busiest area of development on the island. I can count five buildings and a chapel. I know the last remaining tree of the Bardsey Apple is in Nant and I look for a tree in the recess of a high, stone wall.

The ruins of St Mary's Abbey dominate the approach to Nant. The constructions erected by Saint Cadfan in the year 516 were replaced by stone buildings in the thirteenth century. It was to feed the monks that the apple orchard was created. Over the course of a thousand years, as the island's renown spread, and the pilgrims arrived, this orchard grew to cover the lowlands with a thick sprawl of apple trees. Then, in 1537 with the dissolution of the monasteries, the island was taken from the monks and the apple trees were abandoned to the wild. A dark age in the island's history had begun. Pirates and smugglers roamed the shores and fugitives found asylum among the incurious residents. During the tumultuous civil war in the seventeenth century, Parliamentarians held captured Royalists here. As the abbey faded from memory and into ruin, the apple trees persisted, feeding the hungry, the desperate, the criminal and the imprisoned.

Legitimacy dawned again on Bardsey Island with the agricultural settlement in the eighteenth century. Settlers from the Welsh mainland would have encountered an island scarred by history and neglect: a ruined abbey, debris around the shore, the bones of more than just pilgrims and a single, healthy, mature apple tree. Nant was built during this era of settlement. They built around the abbey, next to the apple tree and at the foot of the hill to protect against the unruly sea. I reach this small cluster of buildings. The houses are close together but face away. Companionship and solitude. I see a high stone wall I recognise and a man I do not. He is one of the farmers here. He waves and returns to his haunches pulling weeds from a plant bed. I walk around the wall. The wall surrounds his house. I circle the perimeter and find him again, picking mud from his hand-fork. I ask if the tree is here. 'Was,' he replies. 'Cut it down a few year back.' He looks over to me and shields his eyes from the afternoon sun 'caught a blight. Put the home at risk.' He returns to his haunches and digs again at the plant bed.

Ingrid Fagundez is Brazilian. She studied Journalism in Brazil and was a reporter at *Folha de S.Paulo*, the biggest Brazilian newspaper, and at the BBC. Her writing focuses on subjects such as migration, race, class, family and faith, mainly but not exclusively in her country.

My love, I offer you this

'*Salve,* Negro[1],' he wrote in a formal tone I never heard from him. I was a baby when he died. 'What a beautiful little guy,' he used to say while bouncing me on his knees. He was ill and thought I was a boy.

'*Salve*, Negro,' he wrote to her in 1950, a year before they got married, a year before they kissed for the first time. She keeps his postcards on a table beside her chair, the chair she leaves only to go to bed. 'Good night, Negro,' she must say, shuffling slowly towards the empty bedroom.

'*Salve,*' he penned on a photograph mailed to Brazil, where she lived with her family on a farm. Father, mother, eight brothers and sisters, all dead now. 'What a beautiful little girl,' she says to me. She is ill and thinks

1 'Regards, Negro', in Portuguese

I'm a child.

My grandfather Teodoro married my grandmother Rena in 1951. She is Brazilian. He was Uruguayan. The family carries this dual blood – half Portuguese, half Spanish – as do the letters he sent to her after they met. They lived on different sides of the border and it never became clear to me how they found each other at 21. 'We just did,' my grandmother told me one day. 'My Negrinho,' she continued, mentioning his nickname. '*Mi amor*,' he used to say in the beginning of his letters. A warm start to generally short, generic messages: 'I offer you this photo with all my love wishing you a Happy Christmas and a prosperous New Year with health and happiness.'

The tenderness of my grandfather appears to be in his calligraphy – delicate curves to the right, uppercase in the caring signature – as it was in his eyes, not in his words, according to my mother. A quiet man, indeed. Presents and declarations of affection were rare, other women were not. A common practice at that time, Mom explained. The wife would know about the mistresses but couldn't moan. After all, he was gentle, a hard worker. 'I offer you this, wishing you a Happy Christmas and a prosperous New Year,' my grandmother had written to him four days earlier in the same December 1950. On the other side of the postcard, a picture of a brunette holding a blank page, daydreaming about her suitor. Ladies should be discreet, she advised me once. A silenced woman, indeed.

They exchanged postcards and photos for six months while my grandfather was working in a small city in Uruguay. When he returned, they got married. They had met a few times before the trip, under my Italian great-grandfather's supervision. Negro would walk or pedal to the farm, which had beautiful mulberry trees. My grandmother and her sisters would sit beneath them to watch the mornings go by. I think about the trees, about my grandma's laugh when leaning on them and wonder if they really knew each other. I wonder if Rena and Negro weren't just an engaged couple who had to keep in touch. So they wrote brief lines with good wishes and diplomatic signs of love. Perhaps there was a need to be prudent, an attempt to avoid my great-grandfather's vigilant eyes. Possibly an ignorance of words.

Eventually love became cloudless, loyal to the misleading nature of feelings that build up over time. Reticent love in the old notes, muted love for decades, aged love on my grandmother's hands when she touches the envelopes so softly. She leans on the chair to read the sentences again and again, forgetting what they say after a few seconds, smiling as if there was so much affection then as there is now. Was there?

—

I have a favourite last moment with my grandmother. She is not dead yet, but she is a little less alive with every new day. We are at a park in the border city where we were born, where she spent all her years, from where I escaped so early. It's Sunday. The sky is a blinding blue and a mild wind blows our clothes. From a bench, we watch families eating popcorn. Dogs bark and scare a tiny brown bird that flies away. His wings pass close to our heads before landing on the tree above us. The old dusty leaves still offer good shade and, hidden from the sun, the breeze makes our skin cold. She smiles. 'What a beautiful day! What a beautiful park! Wonderful! Wonderful!' Grandma is happy. She always was, in some way. Not many things made her sad. It had to be truly painful, horrible, irreversible to rip some tears out of her. It happened. That's life, she used to say, already drying her face with a towel. If you want to survive, you can't go down with every argument. 'It's a crazy family, everyone here is nuts,' and she would be laughing again.

Grandma is going down now. I want to ask her what failed in her philosophy, in the principles I've kept in my mind since I was kid. Did she forget to wipe all the tears? Did some of them drip behind her eyes? Maybe they are rotting her inside; large mould patches we can't see. I want to ask her but she doesn't listen to me. She only hears the birds, the dogs and the boy playing football in front of us. 'What a beautiful little boy! What a lovely day!'

We were at the park with my mom and her cousin but I decided to exclude them from this carefully constructed picture. It's just us, beside each other, yelling how wonderful everything is. Despite the pain, the sorrow and death. How wonderful it is to be alive. Grandma was half alive that Sunday but she still could salute it. She had learned this: to be grateful for the smallest joys, not to complain, to grin. I have always admired her good nature in dealing with problems, how she was the only laughter among heavy sighs. I used to nap with her on hot summer afternoons, the bright sunlight leaking through the blinds, and before falling asleep I would stare at her face in adoration. Such a nice grandma, I thought, touching her wrinkles. I would create a story with every one of them, dozens of rivers flowing to the sea, roads to unknown landscapes, scars earned in bloody battles.

I went to sleep in her dark bedroom, on her old bed and woke up today. I woke up to look at grandma one more time and suddenly faced a woman, a woman of the 1950s. A girl who studied until 7th grade, taught by nuns. A kid who drove a wagon to the convent, who still draws her own name. A young lady of one love, who lost it many times. Many times before its final departure. Who lost Grandpa to lovers and a life parallel to three children, low wages and a small wooden house that caught fire, burning everything she owned. Parallel feelings that grandma slowed.

Grandma is about to explode. Not her fragile body, her paper bones, but her head. Part of it is already gone. Dates, names and faces crumble in the rarefied air of her brain. I too am slowly fading away. I affirm my existence, I scream, I expose my freedom and desire. I'm still fading to her.

I have a least favourite moment with my grandmother. Mom and I are getting on the bus to leave the border city, so I call her for one more goodbye. 'Ingrid, I had a beautiful dream,' she says. 'I dreamt you were visiting me and we went to the *parque*. It was such a good day. You see how I'm getting forgetful... I thought it was true.'

—

My grandfather came back in a dream.

He suddenly appeared to celebrate his birthday, smiling and wearing a brown beret. The family was angry. 'Why did you leave for so long?' my uncle cried, letting laughter slip from his lips. Colourful balloons hung over his head while Grandpa stayed silent, as always. He never had a voice to me. Even in my sleep.

The nature of our relationship was immaterial from the beginning. When I was a child, he was the first star that rose in the sky. While dusk took over the day, I would look for him. There he was: big, shiny and distant. I would nod my head to say hello. He acknowledged my earthly being quietly.

As I grew older and nights turned deeper, he became the unreachable man in the photographs. It didn't matter how long I stared at the yellow paper, I could never see him. Only his nicely combed hair, his elegant face and his store, where he made leather products for farmers. There were belts, boots and cells, but no Grandpa. He had no body. My grandfather was the stories about him.

Negro never had a car. He was too poor to buy one and made his way from his *correaria* to the city by bicycle. The store usually occupied the front part of the house where the family was living and his sons helped him sew the leather. Black and white cowhides were suspended from the ceiling and blocked the exterior light, making their work gloomy. The customers were mainly conservative countrymen. Uruguay and Brazil were under military dictatorships and Grandpa thought that was good. He despised the left wing guerrillas: 'Tramps *Tupamaros*,' he would say.

Negro liked things to stay in their places. His moustache was always neatly trimmed, I notice from the pictures. He was very handsome – a film star type, some would suggest – and popular with the ladies. One of his love affairs lasted many years. Mom doesn't recall her name, but she knew it then. So did Grandma. The unnamable woman was a familiar presence, as were the gaps in his accounts. My grandfather lost his wedding ring on a plane trip. When he opened the window to wave at the clouds, the ring fell from his finger, he told. Nobody is sure where he was going or why. I was disappointed the first time I flew. The windows were sadly sealed.

My mother narrated most of my grandfather's tales to me. They were her way of passing through the secrecy, through his muteness. Her monologue about him was the same ever since I can remember: a nice man, forever calm, not very present. A laconic sweetheart. He pedalled his bike on the stone streets, cut the leather with sharp knives and swayed in his rocking chair, smiling. Not a sound. Grandma was there, muttering constantly, putting bandages on everything. She wrapped the past with a red bow, upon which she now weeps forgetful tears. The women in our family are always talking to remain silent. I was too, until I decided to write.

I'm done searching for him. Maybe that's why he has found me. In dreams and thoughts, tarot cards and dear spirits, he talks to me, close for the first time. An inhabitant of my mind, Negro became the symbol of the blank spaces in life, the hereditary voids I cannot occupy. The endurance of a love I can't understand, the reverence I deny, the unspoken words I will never be able to guess. He is the memory of someone I've never met. She is the oblivion of my recollections, dissolving body and psyche. In me there is one last encounter. A perfect union, in the end.

Justus Flair is (probably) moving back to America after two years in Ireland and England. Originally from the centre of the United States, she's planning to head towards a coast – she isn't particular about which coast – and resume working in journalism. Justus tends to explore social issues, culture, and travel in her writing.

Generation of Endlings

*The following excerpt is from a longer piece about
names within the author's family*

I wasn't at my grandma's funeral. But I was in the cemetery's bright June sunshine when we piled dirt on her.

She found permanent rest there, months after her last breath when the ground had been frozen, impenetrable for her stone and remains. No epitaph or grand quote on loss covered her freshly installed memorial marker, a simple burgundy stone with Gloria F Flair and the span of her life in raised gold. On the left, down in the corner, was a penguin. On the right, a wolf. A ribbon in the center let curious passers-by know she was a 'beloved mom, grandma.'

I did love her. She died a week and a day before my birthday. I had her for twenty-three years, less eight days, but what I don't know about her could fill a dozen tomes.

I stared at her name to keep solemn-faced through my evangelical aunt's prayer crammed with too many 'Lord Jesus's and 'Dear God's. Grandma was the last Flair of her generation; the estranged husband who gave her the name is two years buried, though he is as present to me in death as he never was in life.

Those of us standing at her gravesite that day – my sisters Mariah and Reilly, myself, my parents, and my aunt – are the last six Flairs left. Mariah, Reilly, and I are in a morbid marathon to be the Flair endling.

'Endling' is bestowed upon a creature cursed to be the last of its species, a family of one until the name dies out forever. My dad has no sons. My aunt has no children. Neither Mariah nor I plan on reproducing. That leaves Reilly; if she has kids, they are destined to be Flairs in temperament, appearance, and unluckiness only. They'll have a father's name. One of us will live to see every other Flair fade.

But Flair is a good name and I am happy to have it, a gift my father shared with his daughters and our mother. My parents put great care and effort into choosing names to pair with Flair. Their goal was for all three children to make it through school without ever having a classmate with the same name. They made it by the skin of their teeth. Mariah Carey almost ruined their first round, but the other Mariah in our high school was a year behind ours. Reilly comes across Rileys occasionally, but rarely another

Reilly. There was almost a catastrophe with Justus, though. Another girl, my age with my name, was at the middle school over in Riverside. She moved to Des Moines before we ever merged to the same high school, unknowingly averting a crisis. I met her in line at Wal-Mart on Black Friday two years later when she was back visiting family.

I remained the only Justus, not even a Justice in sight until college. My parents breathed a sigh of relief, casting off the worry that they'd have to find something new to call me.

I've always loved my name, been protective of it – correcting misspellings and explaining pronunciation – because I know how close I came to never having it.

My parents occasionally argue about who chose the name. I'm inclined to believe my dad's version; he's always had the better memory of the two and his story is more vivid.

Reading the newspaper the week before I was born, Dad saw the obituary of a man named Justus. The guy was 79 or 81 – Dad couldn't remember which, by the time he spun the tale for me – and he looked like Santa Claus, fluffy full white beard and everything. Right then Dad decided Justus was a good name for his son.

I think Dad was keeping his fingers crossed for a son; not because he's ever seemed less than thrilled with our family of four women, but because he didn't want to tell my mother he hated the name she'd picked out for a girl. Rowan, my maternal grandmother's maiden name, should have become mine. As soon as the doctor induced labor and told them 'It's a girl!' my dad was stuck. He had two options: give his daughter a name he didn't like or enrage a birthing wife.

Mom took the Rowan blow better than expected, possibly aided by pain medication. She was likely livid at Dad's sense of timing, but she had bigger things to worry about at that moment. 'Whatever comes out of me, we're calling Justus.'

I scoured the internet for that life-changing and name-changing obituary when I was twenty-one. Justus R Miller was actually 83 years old. He went by Jus – an abbreviation only my immediate family ever uses for me – and was named after his father, Justus A Miller. He was a lawyer, educated at the same university where I was doing my undergrad. For a hot minute I took it as a sign I should go to law school the next year. Luckily, I didn't follow through. Jus was a Presbyterian and worked as a Military Intelligence special agent during World War II. He had been sick for quite some time and left behind many relatives, including two daughters and zero sons, no third-generation Justus. His home was one hour and two minutes' drive from mine.

There was no picture on the site, so I never saw if he really was a Santa

Claus doppelgänger.

His ancestry wasn't included in the sixty-one lines of newsprint, so I gained no insight into the name's origin. When I moved to Ireland two years later, after graduating from university, I worked with a Bavarian woman who told me the name was German. She'd expected a man when I showed up my first day.

The second of three daughters, I got the name of my parents' first son and I've basked in it every day.

At thirteen, my volleyball team wanted us all to have nicknames to put on our warm-up jackets. Several girls already had one, earned from a killer serve or a running joke or a laughable mishap. I did not. I was made to feel a little embarrassed about it, like I had to do something worthy of a nickname or pick one for myself and plaster it across my shoulders or down my sleeve like everyone else. Wanting to belong, craving that sense of camaraderie, I let my teammates throw out suggestions. Then scorned each. I didn't want to be addressed by something I did on the court or defined by what I did off it, undercutting the authority I had when wearing those blue and white sneakers and blood-stained knee pads. I wanted my name.

I shouldn't have to give up my fantastic name because other people's parents hadn't taken the time to come up with something better. I wasn't sorry for that – I'm still not – and I put my real name across every jersey I had.

Friends have told me I'm too proud of my name. I tell them jealousy is cruel. But it's not pride – I can't be proud of something handed to me, unearned and unworked for – but it is affection and a need to embrace the one thing I've always had.

When I've had nothing to say, I've had a name that people stopped and commented on, questioned, maybe admired. I'm asked to relay the story of where it came from, the underlying enquiry of what kind of people my parents are barely concealed. I endure unfunny jokes about sisters named Liberty and Freedom and keep my eyes unrolled during questions about my artistic flair and flair for the dramatic. But no one else gets those reactions.

It's hard to admit, when people ask, how little I know about my name and genealogy.

I have never met another Flair, outside of those who share my table on Christmas. It is a common word but an uncommon name. I'm completely ignorant of its origin. Farther than two generations back, my family history on the Flair side is a black slate dotted with question marks. Scouring free genealogy sites has taught me that the French Flaire, still rare, is seven times more common. I've speculated that the name is a bastardized spelling, copied sloppily or intentionally changed at Ellis Island, though

I can't even say with certainty that my ancestors arrived in America through the island. The error could have been more severe, a letter changed rather than dropped; Blair is 1,700 times as popular as Flair. Linguistically, the change would make sense.

My friend, who studied linguistics in college, tried to explain it to me. From what I can gather, the b sound is a 'voiced bilabial stop,' which means the vocal chords make the sound and the lips stop it. With an f, an 'unvoiced labiodental fricative,' the teeth and lips make the sound and nothing stops it, it just fades. When you put an unvoiced 'l' sound after a 'b', it can become a fricative, like an f. The 'fl' sound is easier for mouths to form than the 'bl;' it has something to do with the shape of the mouth and the movement of the tongue against the teeth. It is why people tend to pronounce Blair like 'Buh-lair.' Your mouth needs a little help putting the b and l together, so it inserts a vowel sound or chooses an easier consonant. It took a couple attempts to explain that to me, but I think I understood once all the technical vocabulary like 'alveolar lateral position' was stripped away.

The gist was that Flair could have come from Blair because it was easier to say and easily misheard and recorded; that justifies the dozens of times I've heard my mom say, '*Flair*, F like Frank,' into the phone. My surname could be a mistake born of laziness and a lack of outspoken pride in my ancestors.

But not Justus. Justus took a lot of thought and debate between my parents. They couldn't lightly give out a homophone of one of the most revered words in the English language, a word chanted through streets in protest and used as a rally cry, pairing it with a surname that, by definition, boasts of instinctive aptitude and ability – with 'genius' as a synonym, no less.

If 'Justus Rowan Flair' wasn't so unfortunate sounding, perhaps I could have taken on both names. But instead the simple, bland Anne was sandwiched between my names, used only on legal documents where it is an obligation, not a joy.

Anne is a disruption, a break in the flow of Justus Flair. It's as if my parents poured all their energy and thought into our first names, then just gave my sisters and me their own middle names.

It's a bit backwards. I believe middle names are often the name parents were too afraid to give children, a name they worried might be too 'out there' or a family name deemed too formal for a forename.

I'm glad Mom and Dad weren't too nervous or conservative to choose bold names; I feel insurmountably lucky that my parents took their first act of raising me – figuring out what to call me – so seriously.

I make continual attempts to justify my claim to names I never asked for but have claimed wholeheartedly and shamelessly. Nevertheless, sometimes I wonder if it was the right decision. I don't mean that my parents might regret the name, that I might not have lived up to it in their eyes. Rather that even when preening like a cockatiel with a mirror over Justus Flair, I occasionally feel crushing guilt for not being Rowan Flair.

Peter Goulding is a climber from the North of England. For the last ten years he has been a self-employed millwright: a fixer of windmills. He is currently writing *SLATEHEAD: the Punks who climbed The Slate and made it great.*

Slatehead

Why did I fall so hard for climbing on slate? Maybe I thought it liked me. It was letting me move in a beautiful way, it felt good, and we looked good together. I got compliments the first time I went into the quarries – people I respected, hard climbers, called me 'nails' and said I was taking to it 'like a duck to water.'

'So you're a slatehead now then?' someone asked. I didn't know the word, but I was.

—

In the back of the *Llanberis Slate* guidebook is a list of all the routes in the quarries, with who climbed them and on what date. There are forty pages' worth. Someone must have spent hours going through the new routes books to make this list. Frankly, I couldn't care less. It's nothing to me who climbed what, when. All I care about is what I am going to climb next.

Although, saying that, there are a couple of pictures at the front, of some 1960s climbers. One of them shows about six men, standing on each other's shoulders to start a climb; they are all obviously pissing themselves laughing about it, a fun mess around with mates.

Immediately above the picture is an entry:

1969 June 10 Bluebottle R Kane, J Brazington.

That's a funny name, Brazington. And I've heard it before.

In our house in Liverpool there was a heavy white helmet, which I used to take from my dad's wardrobe because I liked soldiers and wearing it while jumping down the stairs made me feel like a paratrooper. It was Dad's climbing helmet, with hard leather straps which bit into the skin under your chin. The enamel on the top was scuffed and scratched and there was a maker's badge stuck inside, cloth, red-purple with gold letters. I can't remember the maker's name, but Dad had written P. GOULDING across the edge of the label with biro.

Dad had only climbed for a couple of years in university ten years before I was born, then didn't bother any more. He still spoke about it though; I knew he was, in some way, 'a climber.'

Once, he told me about a friend he had climbed with, John Brazington, whom everyone called Little Brazington.

'He was short but very strong, but he was very afraid when he climbed. He'd get just up off the ground, then freeze. He'd stay there for ages until he pulled himself together, then he'd go and climb it.'

'Was he a coward, Dad?' The way a ten year old thinks, raised on war stories.

'No. He could always make himself do it.'

One night at a party, someone changed the music on the record player and Brazington didn't like it. He broke a pint glass over the bloke's head, who went down like a sack of coal. In the morning, Brazington went to the police station to hand himself in, believing he'd killed the man. The police told him to fuck off, no one was dead that they knew of.

Dad and I watched films together. My first memory was seeing *Duel* – Spielberg's first film – with him. I'd not been able to sleep, and went down and he let me stay up to watch it: I liked the truck in it. One night we watched the famous climber Catherine Destivelle soloing: climbing without ropes, hundreds and hundreds of metres from the ground, on African sandstone the colour of honey in the evening sun. She wore green lycra shorts, and she was beautiful. Long tanned limbs, curly hair, brown streaked with blonde from the sun. The movement across the rock, totally fearless and graceful. No hanging around, arguing with herself about whether to go for it, she just moved up the rock as if it was a dance.

Dad shouted the first time she hung upside down from her feet and hands. I kept on shouting every time she moved. Dad said 'shut up, will you.' I had thought he would approve, I was just copying him.

I can't ask Dad about John Brazington. For one thing, in June 1969, when Bluebottle was climbed, Dad was nowhere near North Wales: that summer, he and his mate Neil drove a knackered van from Europe through Iran and into Afghanistan, just for the crack of it. Dad had stopped climbing by then.

For another thing, Dad is dead, bowel cancer at age 53, when I was 25. Killed by his diet, everything out of a tin and never a lettuce in sight. He thought the stomach pains were because onions gave him indigestion, or maybe he was drinking tea too strong. For fuck's sake.

I saw a photo of him from the spring before he was diagnosed and can't believe I didn't notice. I was just back from Australia, so I had a tan, but he was white. White skin, white hair. Maybe I just thought he was getting old: actually, he was bleeding into his guts, becoming anaemic, while little clumps of endlessly replicating cells swam around his bloodstream, lodging where they could and setting up house in his lungs, his stomach, his kidneys and – fatally – his liver.

Mum and Dad met at Liverpool University through the climbing club. The climbing wall was in the university sports centre, we walked past it when Mum took me and my sisters swimming there. The climbing wall frightened and fascinated me. It was made of dark grey, blue-black concrete, cast pillars and buttresses, ruined fortifications from the castle of Llyr. They hung out of the wall above the badminton courts.

You got to the changing rooms for the pool by walking along a raised walkway, so we were level with the top third of these columns. I looked over the railing, and it added to the fear. Sometimes there were climbers there, often on the middle column, hanging from their red ropes as they belayed their partners up to meet them. Rarely, there was someone trying the right-hand third of the wall with much smaller blocks and featureless gargoyles sticking out, but I never saw anyone on the left-hand line, which was no more than dents and sharp shallow bulges in the concrete.

That was the hardest one, Mum told me.

'Can I go on it one day?'

'Ask your dad. He might take you.'

He never would. He hated it. It was a waste of time, and dangerous. I overheard him once at the kitchen table counting up: eight dead. He had a picture of him climbing something in Wales called the Sickle, Dad is sitting on a rock with a hook nose and curly hair under his climbing helmet.

Dad pointed at the leading climber and said, 'That lad is dead now. He got hit by a rock in the Alps.' It didn't mean anything to me. The picture was in black and white. I could tell the belayer was my dad though, his hands out front paying the rope out, by the way he has his sleeves rolled. He always had them rolled into a flat rectangle a bit above the elbow, gingery-gold hairs running up his arm and freckles that faded and stopped where his shirt blocked the sun. When I looked at the ash we got back from the crematorium, I couldn't believe that the freckles were gone.

The lead climber, it turns out when I check with my mum, is John Brazington.

Ten years after Dad died, Mum is sitting there, and has picked up the only book I want to read: *One Day as a Tiger,* about Alex MacIntyre, Dirty Alex, who was killed in the mid-eighties by a single stone which fell from Annapurna's south face. It's been recently written by John Porter, twenty-five odd years after his mate died.

I start to plan how I can get the book off her – divert her with a gardening book perhaps – when she speaks up.

'Ooh. Al Rouse. I knew him.'

I look at her. Al Rouse was a serious climber, one of the best ever, who died on K2 after being the first Brit to summit it.

'What are you on about now, Mother?'

'Al Rouse. Your dad and me climbed with him in Liverpool.'

'Not possible, I am afraid, Mother. Al Rouse went to Cambridge. Famously. Your wits are addled.'

'It says that here, but he was from Liverpool, he must have been in Merseyside Climbing Club. We didn't know him well, just to say hello to.'

I quickly check on Wikipedia and am furious to find out she's right.

'Ooh look, Mike Hammill. I knew him, too. He was hard, one of the hard climbers. He had a face like a sledgehammer. I've told you about him, he was from Sheffield, he was always on about Stanage. Stanage, Stanage, Stanage.'

I consider. She turns a page in the book.

'Any other famous climbers you know, Mother? Chris Bonington perhaps?'

'Who's he?'

I give up. I think for a while.

'What was Dad like as a climber, Mum?'

She drops the book and looks up into the air.

'Well. Quite good, I think. I remember him doing *Cemetery Gates*, everyone seemed quite impressed. He got bored, of course. A lot of the men were very macho, macho types who couldn't make it with women. Then in his third year he knuckled down to work a bit, and of course he was going out with me, so we spent all our time together.'

I pick up my slate guidebook.

'Is this someone he climbed with Mum? J Brazington?'

'Yes. John. He went out with your Auntie Nica. She worked at Plas-y-Brenin one summer. John was one of the macho types, he couldn't believe his luck with Nica, and they weren't together long.' Auntie Nica was glam.

'Well who's with him? R Kane?'

'Yes. Rick Kane. He was lovely. Very quiet, lovely lad. Always wore nice jumpers. It was terrible when he died.'

She looks at the book.

'Funny. They never really climbed together, they weren't much like each other. Maybe it's not the same ones.'

'Brazington and Kane? Look at the names. It'd be a bit of coincidence, don't you think?'

I give up again.

Dad didn't like climbing because of the mortality rate at the time. Climbers in the late sixties could and did die. The gear was only starting the long journey to standardised high quality and rigorous testing. At the top level, many of that generation climbed themselves into extinction. So in Dad's head climbing was lethal, made more lethal by car crashes on the fast roads and blind corners heading into North Wales.

When I get on the slate, people tell me I am nails: I'm not really. I get scared, but I can keep a lid on it, or flush the fear away and operate. I detach, and watch myself do things from far, far away. As I climb more, the situations that I find frightening recede, and so I need to climb harder to seek them out, pushing the fine boundary of what is too frightening ever to try and what will leave me unmoved.

On the *State of the Heart*, I slip and my handholds are bad, in an awkward position. My strength is failing – a power-bar on a computer game, falling from green to orange to red, and soon nothing left. As my strength starts to weaken, my balance and stability on the slab start to weaken, too. It is not the height or the fall, but the way the fact of it creeps inevitably forward towards me, I can see it coming in a few seconds' time. The fear comes out as words, a babble of unconsidered phrases – 'I'm sorry Dad, I'm sorry Dad,' – then I'm off, and of course, swinging safely on a stainless-steel bolt drilled into the rock.

I ask my mate Lee if he'd heard what I'd said. Lee pretends he can't remember. 'Oh, you were just talking nonsense, mate.' I love him for that.

J Brazington, a name in a book.

Peiyi Li is a native Cantonese from Southeast China who lived in Cologne, Germany for a year before she moved to Norwich. A trilingual and a traveller, she is keen on exploring multiple cultures and languages. She sees herself as a Eurasian and hopes someday to open a chip store in China (a potential name: Timmy Chips).

Scooter Rider in a Suit

For my potential future husband, the twenty-one-year-old me decided to skip university classes for three weeks, losing the marks that were guaranteed by attendance to be there for my Mr Aussie's time in China.

It was mid-October, 2016. The young man I had missed for months showed up in my hometown of Dongguan, a coastal city near Hong Kong in Southeast China. During the next three days I kept pointing out different architectural styles to my dear John, from wooden pagodas built during the Ming Dynasty[2] and formal gardens in the Qing Dynasty[3], to skyscrapers in the shape of a rocket or a modem.

Then we began to travel, past more skyscrapers and more wide roads packed with traffic in neighbouring Shenzhen, an important megacity with a population of sixteen million. Next, we saw honking scooters flying around numerous construction sites in Nanchang, the capital city of an inland province north of Canton, before we reached Wuyuan, a rural county six hundred and fifty miles northeast of my hometown, hidden in forests and mountains.

After we got off the train, when we were walking towards the exit of the station, we saw a large crowd of the local people waiting outside, making us feel like we had landed in a major international airport instead. This hadn't occurred to us previously, nor did it look familiar to me in my experience about Chinese train stations. The moment we stepped out with other arriving passengers, the stillness of the crowd was broken into a nearly attack from numerous ignited leopards. Within seconds we were enveloped by them, who were trying to sell their guest houses and driving services to us, all talking loud and fast.

John was terrified, not able to walk at all. I held his hand tightly to assure him that everything was OK and had to drag him out of the crowd. 'Bú yòng le xìe xìe,' I rejected their offers politely whilst walking past them. I could have just ignored them without saying anything, but I wouldn't like them to see us as arrogant toffs either.

But they wouldn't let me leave that easily. With controlled desperation they inquired – 'Little girl, where is he from?'

2 Ming Dynasty in Chinese ancient history: 1368–1644
3 Qing Dynasty in Chinese ancient history: 1644–1912

Later I learnt from the owner of my guest house, who was in her mid-thirties, that John was the third foreigner she had met in person during her life in Wuyuan. She still found her encounter with the first two foreigners during the previous summer hard to believe. 'It's understandable if they are hanging out in big cities like Beijing and Shanghai, but here in Wuyuan? No way!' she giggled.

'How good-looking he is,' she remarked after a while.

Seemingly as an afterthought she added, 'You are as well.'

I thanked her. Though I knew it was a compliment, I was slightly annoyed. What if I wasn't considered pretty?

Like that woman, many people in the inland parts of China that are less known to the world would have met foreigners only once or twice in their lives, which made travelling in these remote areas extremely difficult for foreigners. Although places like Wuyuan became popular tourist attractions for townspeople recently, there was zero English written on signs at bus stops or guest houses. Most local people in Wuyuan, as I noticed, were above thirties, who didn't grow up having English lessons, and their children, who did speak some, were studying or working in the cities nearby. As the tourism development here was still in the early stage, shambolism still existed. For instance, John still couldn't figure out how come it could be one third cheaper to stay with our guest house lady as 'her relatives' instead of 'tourists'. I was a little reluctant to explain it to him even though I spoke the language; I didn't want him to think the Chinese, and me, are dishonest people.

What made things more complicated was that I was travelling with a tall white guy. Wherever we went, people were naturally drawn to John's finely-chiselled face. 'What do they think of me?' Noticing their discreet observation, John asked, forcing a smile. 'A rich white guy?'

I was embarrassed, but before I had time to respond to him I noticed myself being observed as well. Once they had ascertained that I was East Asian like them, their eyes would move downward from mine. Some of them, I suspected, might have been silently accusing me of 'selling out' to a westerner simply because he was better looking. Others might have been jealous, then decided that it was not true love and that I was just with him for free English lessons and even a chance to live abroad.

Perhaps this explained why I liked this isolated mountain so much. To avoid people we decided on our second day in Wuyuan to climb a mountain only known to the locals. It proved to be a right choice – it was the first quiet place we had been in the entire week. All it had was a rugged stone path dotted in mud, shaded by the surrounding forest in different hues of green, light spots dancing in between. There was no one else but us.

We chatted as we climbed the path. John started to share his family stories from Australia again, which I enjoyed a lot. It was one of those rare moments during this trip when I didn't need to be a spokesperson for China, but just a listener to someone I cared for. He had often mentioned his family, particularly one of his elder sisters, since we first met four months ago in July, in Cologne, Germany where I had studied and lived for a year. It was nice to see that he valued family too – the impression my dad had of westerners was somewhat the opposite.

'My sister didn't go to college right after senior high,' John recalled, 'She worked in a farm for some time. Lots of cows and sheep there. I will show you around there when you visit. It is really cool.'

'Wow,' I responded, 'I imagine she must be the queen of cow!'

'You said my sister was a cow!' John burst out, looking daggers at me.

The air seemed to freeze. I apologised immediately, saying it really was meant to be a compliment. 'Your sister must be able to ride. It is really cool, like a cowboy in old western movies, you know, and they are such beautiful animals, you know...'

'I know.'

I reached for his hand and said sorry again.

We didn't talk for a long while. I felt very bad for not having known about this taboo word before. For the Chinese, cows are very important in our agriculture-based civilisation. Their male counterpart, the oxen, is one of our twelve zodiac signs! These animals are strong, docile, with large watery eyes and never complaining about hard work, which makes them our nation's favourite animals. Even when the term is used to refer to women, it symbolises nourishment and maternity, qualities that our culture values in them. How come it became insulting in English?

I didn't tell John about this though, for fear of triggering a bigger fight. Earlier, before we set off, we had argued about the state of our relationship. He would fly back to Australia at the end of the journey, whilst I didn't want to give up on my plan of returning to Europe. No commitment had been forthcoming. No promise would be given. An air of uncertainty hung over us, like a dark cloud.

The China trip wasn't really for me. John had already planned for it to end his gap year in grandeur, even before we met in Cologne. In July, we spent two days together, the chat flowing like champagne. This was followed by a week of travelling from Milan to Florence in August, during which he bought me gelato every day. When we saw each other again in October I almost cried. In July, I hadn't foreseen that he would become, if only for a moment, the sole person in China who could relate to the European part of me. A random traveller bringing me a seashell, a pocket

Aussie slang dictionary and a soft toy koala, pleading for my time in a broken voice. I couldn't say no.

From then on, we had tried to avoid quarrels of any kind, worried that they could instigate the downfall of our romance. I used to think that fighting was the biggest enemy of a relationship, but now it had become a privilege, unaffordable to us.

By the time we reached the mountain top and finished our lunch in its small village, it was already two in the afternoon. The locals said that the stone footpath we had taken was the only way downhill. 'Or,' they suggested, 'you can take a scooter taxi. We can help order one for you. Then you will be taking a cement road. But it will be a bit bumpy as it is still being built... Where is he from?'

I agreed and thanked them for their help, but before I finished explaining it to John I was caught up by the same old question. 'He's from Australia,' I answered quickly, not wanting to appear rude. While I was doing all the talking, the Aussie was inhaling the aroma of the green tea they had made him and examining the house where we had our lunch, which in fact was prepared by the old couple who lived there since there was no restaurant. Like other houses in this village, it was a spacious brick house that wasn't whitewashed. The walls and the floors were all bare, in old brown cement. The lighting in their living room didn't have lampshades.

The scooter taxi arrived and its rider, Cheng, greeted us with a toothy smile. The scooter had an extended backseat to fit two more people, over which hung a yellow plastic weatherproof shelter. Cheng seemed to be in his late fifties, tall and stout with broad shoulders and smiley mono-lid eyes. His brown cheeks were slightly burnt by the scorching sun, his forehead covered with a film of sweat. Despite the unbearably hot weather, however, he was wearing a loose white shirt and an oversized black suit, with a pair of old but very clean black leather shoes. He looked more like an officer or a business man working in the city than a scooter rider from the countryside.

But his helmet didn't seem to be a good fit at first sight. Rather than something for a professional rider, it was one of those cheap bright yellow helmets made of hard plastic, specifically for construction site workers. Although weird, it made a very delightful picture with the suit.

We said goodbye to the villagers and got on the scooter. I was seated between Cheng and John. The ride lasted for about forty minutes, during which Cheng narrated almost his entire life to me, his yellow helmet bumping all along the journey. I tried talking to John on occasion, but Cheng always chipped in with his life stories, and I felt obliged to listen. Eventually, John gave up talking to me and started to take photographs with his camera.

At the end of the ride, he asked Cheng if he could take some photographs of him. That surprised Cheng a lot at first, but he agreed. In the next five minutes, he tried to look into the lens, giving John a quiet, shy smile. Afterwards he gave us his phone number in case we needed any help in Wuyuan.

That evening John asked what Cheng had told me.

'He came from that village on the mountain top where we had lunch but fifty years ago he moved downhill with his family when he was little, with trolleys because they didn't have a scooter then,' I recalled. 'He went to Shanghai for work after he grew up, which is a seven-hour trip by coach away. That was in the eighties. His first job was projecting films in the cinema. Five years later he opened his own photo studio. In Shanghai he met his wife, who also came from Wuyuan.'

'That sounds really cool.'

'Soon they had their son, but he was born with heart disease. He said it was because they had no money for good food during the pregnancy. They worked extremely hard in the past twenty years to afford the treatment. Luckily the disease had been cured. The son graduated from an art academy last year and since then has been working in Shanghai too.'

'Nice.'

'But he seemed to be troubled with his wife now. He said she preferred Shanghai, but it is not a good place for his bad health so he came back alone. Now they barely talk.'

'Oh.'

I went to the toilet and brushed my teeth for bed. I looked up and studied my face in the mirror, wondering how much underneath could be truly comprehended by the Aussie. I continued to think about Cheng. Cool? Cool to manage a photo studio in Shanghai, a megacity where twenty five million people are struggling to live? Cool to stay marginal and speak with an accent that was not prevalent? Cool to travel between two places excessively in the past thirty years? He had such a tiring time and paid such a cost! The metropolis in his suit, the countryside in his helmet, a juxtaposition that couldn't be more bizarre.

But isn't this what my parents experienced in their early years too? Would he be able to understand?

Once again, I swallowed my stories back.

Later, as we cuddled to sleep, I felt that his feet were cold. His legs too. Perhaps the evenings in this mountainous area were too cool for him. I held him tighter, trying to warm him up. Dub, dub, his heart was beating with mine. I saw a cow mooing in a rolling meadow, lost from the herd.

Yin F Lim was a journalist for 16 years in Malaysia before moving to the UK in 2006. Her writing taps into her interest in food, family stories and the East Asian diaspora. She is working on a memoir about her grandparents' migration from China to colonial Malaya, writing from her perspective as an emigrant herself. Read more on her blog: https://yinflim.com

Have You Eaten

A large bowl sits on the table, filled to the brim. Yellow noodles lie half-submerged in a broth of startling orange, with swirls of coconut milk forming a paisley-like pattern. A mound of cucumber and bean sprouts fills part of the bowl, along with pink-veined prawns and deep-fried tofu puffs cut to expose their spongy insides.

I'm trying hard not to stare at the curry *laksa* the waitress has just put in front of the diner next to us. But with the tables and chairs at C & R Café placed at elbow-jostling distance, it's impossible to ignore the tantalising smell of coconut and chilli wafting from the bowl of noodles. Already, I'm anticipating the magical explosion of warm spiciness as soon as I bite into a piece of curry-soaked tofu.

'So, what are you having?' Nick, my husband, asks as he scans the menu, flicking it with his thumb. 'Why don't you try the *mee Siam*?'

'Hmmm... I don't know,' I dither, taking a surreptitious glance at our neighbour's bowl. 'That guy's curry *laksa* looks so good, but I don't know if I can finish it.'

'How about you?' I throw the question back at Nick, hoping he'd order the *laksa* so I can steal a few bites.

'You know I usually have my *Hokkien mee* but yeah, that looks good...' he trails off, his eyes also straying towards the noodles. We continue discussing the menu when suddenly a stranger's voice interrupts us.

'Don't order it.'

Having overheard us, our dining neighbour couldn't resist offering his opinion. 'I've heard so much about the *laksa* here but really, it's not that great. It's much better back home,' he says, before downing a spoonful of curry broth. Nick and I exchange a quick look. We both think C & R has the best *laksa* in London, having tried it on previous visits.

'No*lah*, it's not that bad,' Nick responds, starting an animated discussion about *laksa*; what makes a good one and where to find it. By the time our noodles arrive – Nick's smoky lard- and soy-flavoured *Hokkien mee* and my *mee Siam* with its sweet-sour tamarind and bean sauce – the three of us are debating about whether the food is better in our homeland of Malaysia, or in Singapore, where our newfound acquaintance is from.

I look around the brightly-lit café, taking in the mix of English and

Malay spoken in the conversations around us, with a smattering of Chinese and Indian dialects. Loud pop music blares from hidden speakers as the waiting staff holler at each other with their orders. It's like being in a busy hawker food centre in Southeast Asia, so much so that when we finally leave, it feels strange to walk into London's cool autumnal air instead of sweltering tropical heat.

As we head towards Chinatown, I ask Nick what he thought about our dining neighbour, and what he had said about the *laksa*.

'*Aiya*, of course he would say the ones at home are better,' Nick replies. 'He's going back there soon.' I nod, agreeing. 'For those of us living here, the *laksa* is pretty good. Beggars can't be choosers.'

'So, shall we pack some food to take home with us?' my husband says as we walk past a restaurant window displaying a row of Cantonese roast duck, its crispy skin glistening in the light.

—

Sudah makan?

That's how we greet each other back in the homeland; not by asking 'how are you' but 'have you eaten'. When we're not eating, we're talking about food. In fact, we're often talking about it while eating: Who makes the best *laksa*. Where to find the best *roti*. What we're going to eat next.

'You Malaysians are the ultimate foodies!' An English friend once said in amused exasperation while listening to us.

We can't help it; we believe we have the best cuisine in the world. 'A spectacular gastronomic experience like no other' is how a Lonely Planet guidebook once described it. A distinct cuisine that's best explained using the Malay word *rojak* meaning 'mixture', which aptly captures the cross-cultural influences of the diverse communities that make up the country – Malay, Chinese, Indian, Eurasian. A cuisine of unique hybrid dishes like curry *laksa*, which marries the South Indian spices of coriander, cumin and curry leaves with Chinese egg noodles, tofu, and coconut milk found locally. Or *ayam Kapitan*, a Malay-Chinese fusion chicken curry flavoured with citrusy lemongrass and kaffir lime leaves, the heat of chilli, and deep savouriness of *belacan* or dried shrimp paste.

Thinking about the food I grew up with often makes me homesick and hungry. Like the other day, when I was dreaming of some *roti jala* soaked in chicken curry. I could almost taste the egg and coconut-flavoured pancake blending with spicy slivers of chicken, the hint of turmeric and curry leaf tingling on my tongue. It was enough to send me to the kitchen at 10am to see what I could have for lunch. Opening the fridge door, all I could find was a tub of yoghurt standing guard over a block of cheese and a woeful wedge of chicken pie left over from the previous night's dinner. As I stared at a wrinkled satsuma half-hidden behind the yoghurt, I wished I could drive to C & R instead. But London was two hours away, a long journey to make just because I was craving familiar food.

By mid-afternoon my longing for some *roti jala* had become so great that I started to Google for a recipe. There were plenty to choose from the large number of Malaysian food blogs online and I picked one that looked the easiest, with the shortest list of ingredients. Soon I was standing over the frying pan, struggling to create the lace-like pancake. There was more of the pale yellow batter on the stove than in the pan, making me wonder if I should just boil some rice instead, to go with the pot of chicken curry that was simmering over the fire. The chicken curry I had made from one of the pre-cooked pastes that are a real boon to less able cooks like myself. Just add meat or vegetables, potatoes, oil, coconut milk, and dinner is on the table in the time it would have taken my mother-in-law to prepare the *rempah* – a spice mix of shallots, chilli, candlenut, garlic, galangal, and turmeric – for hers.

'Hmm... this one's not bad; doesn't have a strong processed taste,' remarked resident curry connoisseur Nick at dinner. Our teenage son Khay, normally a picky eater, wolfed down a plateful of rice with three pieces of coconut-creamy chicken. I bit into one that was nearly falling off its bones and agreed with Nick. It lacked the freshness of the *rempah*-based curry my mother-in-law would make, but it was like quenching your thirst on a terribly hot day with a bottle of lukewarm water because you couldn't find an ice-cold one. Beggars can't be choosers, as my husband would say.

—

'I'm in Chinatown. What do you want for dinner?'

Nick's on the phone from London. He's making his way to the station to catch his train back to Norwich but first, a detour to pick up some food. Several hours later, he's home with containers of *nasi lemak* – coconut-infused rice with fried anchovies and spicy *sambal* – and one of my childhood favourites: *wah tan hor* or braised rice noodles. I catch a whiff of its fragrant prawn and egg gravy as it is being warmed up in the microwave oven, which makes me even more impatient for dinner.

Whenever Nick is in London, he often insists on bringing home our dinner in takeaway boxes, even though I tell him he needn't trouble himself with carrying all that food on the train.

'It's not a problem,' he'll say. 'Then you won't need to worry about what to cook.'

It's more like he won't need to eat my cooking; the thought crosses my mind, followed by guilt for seeming ungrateful. It's true that I struggle with making the family's meals, as cooking has never come naturally to me. But I'm also trying to feed three people with very different palates: if we're having pasta at home, one prefers *fusilli* while the other doesn't want anything but *spaghetti*, and I end up having to eat either although I would much rather have *tortellini*.

There are also days when Nick's attachment to Malaysian or Chinese food can get too much for me. Like when he picks desultorily at the seafood stew I've cooked from a Nigella recipe, then proceeds to make himself a bowl of instant noodles a couple of hours later. Or when we always eat at the same places whenever we're in London.

'There's more to London than just C & R or Chinatown!' exasperated, I tell Nick on a recent trip. 'There's so much variety here: British, Japanese, Spanish, Italian, Brazilian... why don't we try something new?'

'But the food tastes terrible everywhere else,' he replies, grimacing.

'No, it doesn't!' Khay and I protest.

'Fine then, you can eat what you want. I'm going to Chinatown.'

It's not the first time we've had this argument. Usually I end up giving in because I feel we should eat together, and we'll all troop off to Nick's restaurant of choice with our son grumbling about how 'we're having Malaysian food, again.' But this time I decide to stand my ground.

'OK, fine. Khay, where shall we go?'

Later, when we're having sushi and chicken *katsu* at a Japanese restaurant, I wonder about Nick's stubbornness. What is it about the food we grew up with that makes it so irresistible, especially when we're far away from our birthplace?

—

I close my eyes to savour the texture of the bouncy fish paste contrasting with the smoothness of the silky tofu. My taste buds pick up the sweetness of the minced prawn that's been added to the paste, and the saltiness of the soup in which the *yong tau foo* is cooked. I can hear the clatter of utensils and the clanging of pots as the hawker stall owner pours a steaming ladle of hot soup over a bowl of fish-stuffed tofu and vegetables. I can feel the heat emanating from his stove and the humidity enveloping me as trickles of sweat start to form on my hairline. Across the table, my mother is taking a bite of her *wonton mee* while making sure my toddler brother is eating his chicken rice. On my left, my younger brother is drinking sugar cane juice with a straw, his noisy slurps ringing in my ear.

'So, what do you think? Does it taste like the real thing?'

Nick's question pulls me back to present-day Norwich. I open my eyes to see my husband looking expectantly as he awaits my verdict on the food he's spent all morning preparing. I smile and nod, and his face relaxes. It's not the buttery crumbs of Proust's *madeleine* but the savoury taste of *yong tau foo* that's transported me back to my childhood, to family meals at hawker food centres.

Perhaps this is the main reason we are so drawn to our food. We cook and eat to evoke a life left behind and to maintain a connection to our homeland. Grilling chunks of meat at barbecues, the cool summer air redolent with lemongrass and chilli and fingers sticky with peanut dipping sauce, to recreate the smoky atmosphere of the *satay* stalls back home. Cooking pots of *assam laksa* to return to evenings spent with friends slurping rice noodles in sour fishy broth while fighting over the last dollop of pungent prawn paste to enhance the dish.

I once read about how migrants are more likely to abandon their native language than change their diets in their new homes. Somehow, this doesn't surprise me at all.

Jess Morgan is a musician and a writer of songs, described as *gritty British love stories, full of sadness and bite.* Jess has also written for *Oh Comely, Make, The Cardiff Review* and *L'Éphémère Review.* Jess joined the MA Creative Non-Fiction course to write more, to try more and to find different ways of telling stories.

This is the way we walk now

The journey takes twenty minutes – non-stop. The trains that come through are the old ones, with sooty windows, a smell of stale cigarette smoke and BO. The track is more or less parallel to the road, you see them if you're driving. Never more than two carriages, they look like runaways – like trains that have gone mad and escaped from the back of a line of regimented brother and sister carriages, slipped off at the signals and fled to the coast. Running on momentum they dwindle over the last stretch. It's been ten years since I've been on one. But that's still what they look like – these odd, old, slow trains under big skies with painterly clouds.

Great Yarmouth station feels familiar; the unlit waiting area with an unmanned snack kiosk. There is still the cavernous, dirty ceiling with ratty grey feathers caught in the metal grates overhead.

Through the iron bridge to North Quay and left – is the best route into town. Back when this was a regular outing, we'd walk through the right-most section of the bridge. You could see down to the choppy brown water through the gaps between wooden slats. That section is fenced off now. I lean up against the wire and peer in. All the wood and the iron work has a green tinge and a slickness about it that glistens dangerously even in the dim light. I hear the low, seedy cooing of pigeons nestled in the nooks. The left side has been newly painted, in a coat of cadmium red paint. A first-choice red for flags and football tops, glosses over its rivets and girders and the sun skips along the bumps of the metal. This is the way we walk now.

A short man in chef's whites waters the window-boxes of a seafood restaurant, the first visible building on the North Quay, from this direction. He has curly grey hair and thick black eyebrows that seem to emphasise his disdain at the mountain of cans and bottles he has swept into a pile on the doorstep, cider bottles and energy drinks. The window-boxes drip water over pretty Greek-style mouldings. Just small jobs from a long list perhaps, for before their supplier – of thirty-nine years – delivers the day's fresh fish from Lowestoft.

A new blue plaque congratulates Mrs Kikis, the owner of the restaurant for having spearheaded funding efforts for the restoration of the bridge. I had seen the newspaper's report. Mrs Kikis wore a proud expression and a bright red twin-set that matched both her lipstick and the new lacquer of her bridge. She had the look of someone immensely fierce of heart. The local paper reported that forty people came to watch Mrs Kikis cut the ribbon – but also that a local cyclist passing through quickly became the recipient of rapturous applause. He may have inadvertently stolen her thunder.

—

The busiest street in town – the one teeming with families, souvenirs, balloons and mobility scooters on any summer day – is Regent Road. The town's most famous street links the seafront with the bus station and was always the best place to buy a bucket and spade, or a stick of Great Yarmouth rock. A shop that sells County and Western records blasts out standards sung by unknown singers, over steel guitar and the four-to-the-floor provided by the drum-loops of a Casio keyboard.

It's November though now, and most of the shops are closed. I have the run of the street. A big man in a sit-down scooter glides down the middle and throws a tennis ball to a black labrador. He wears a Panama hat which seems a risk. Maybe the dog is trained to fetch it if it blows away on a windy day. He waves to a group of ladies sitting drinking coffee, squashing their necks into their fleece coats outside a café. It has neon signs and La Continental written in gentle, loopy script. It has always looked to me, like something from a film. It's a huge thrill that on a quiet day just like this, alone, I can finally go in.

There is booth seating along the back wall, and a lot of bistro tables inside – though there are far more people sitting at the tables outside where they can smoke. Modelled on an Italian style café, I imagine the place would have been quite chic once. The queue lanes are roped off in the way that museum exhibits are, with a gold velvet rope. The long counter feels immediately exotic. It feels satisfying, sliding a tray along from one end to the till at the other. A machine makes frothy beige lattes in slim transparent glasses. I ask for tea, and to have it in a mug because my hands are still freezing.

I find the outside area silent. The fleece-top women draw back deeply from their cigarettes against the cold. The scampering dog has finally come to rest and I lean back in my chair as if on a Mediterranean terrace, looking at the wide expanse of empty street, boarded-up premises and the brickwork guts of a building that used to be a bowling alley. One of my best friends had a birthday there one year. She was so drunk she bowled the ball in a shocking diagonal that made us each hold in an uncomfortable chestful of gasped air – until she'd hit a strike, three lanes over.

We flew around Gorleston, Yarmouth and the coastal villages then in either a brown, square shouldered Escort, a Fiat Panda in its classic terracotta or my boyfriend's blue-rinse Nova; cars that needed the choke pulling out and a cassette tape pushing in. And we were terrifying drivers. My favourite of the fleet was a friend's mint-green Ford Fiesta – the model that had the really slanty roof. I was there when she reversed it into a BMW. I did my best to mop up tears in the front seat as we called her dad from around the corner and the quiet safety of an empty industrial estate.

Bruce Springsteen forged an entire career on those same aspirations that we had, of jumping in a car and escaping. He came from a small town and he wrote songs about beaches with fairgrounds and about friendships and escape. We were in on the pact – to leave the small towns and the old places behind. The trouble with life outside of a song though, was how quickly it could all come crumbling down. One false move and we were on the phone to our parents to come and bail us out.

I was still making mistakes. Maybe it was because I was on Regent Road, not Thunder Road. My false moves kept on coming it seemed, long after those teenage years. And I was back once more, at the start.

I examine the bones of the bowling alley expecting at any minute to feel a surge of sadness. It looks as if a cherry-picker has lowered from the sky and simply ripped the building up in one scrape. Claws on wires like that, only smaller, still lurk inside glass cases on the seafront, tempting people to play in a twenty-pence piece, blaring obnoxious jingles.

There is something calm and maybe even reassuring, about those raggedy edges. Perhaps it is the clean blue sky you can see through the gap. A flawless sky on a cold day; sturdy, and constant.

After a while, a Greek man prods the people at the table to my right – saying he hasn't seen them there in a while. 'You've been up at Costa!' he teases. Everyone laughs. I watch the two ladies chain-smoking over their tall coffees – yelling out at friends walking down the street. They do this three or four times – and no one is in too much of a rush anywhere that they can't stop.

—

Before I have to double back to the library, I loop quickly around the cinema. During my lifetime it has always been The Hollywood and, for the most part, a leaky roof meant that you could sit on only one side of the main auditorium. My mum and I watched a film there once. We took a bag of microwave popcorn from home. We didn't often do things, just the two of us. It felt so unlike anything else, I would take in everything. I watched her in the cinema light, in profile. You could just make out where her nose was copiously freckled, slightly broken, and all the more beautiful for it. We had forgotten to sit on the dry side and it started to rain. I remember getting dripped on as my mum laughed at all the clever jokes, on her own.

Around the back, the old branding of Rosie's nightclub peeks through the black paint above the windows. The cinema takes up the front part of the building and the club has the back and has its own separate entrance. We used to have our sixth form college parties there, taking it in turns to be sick outside. It has recently become a lap dancing club. This side of the Britannia Pier, the attractions thin out into a long stretch of beach. The wind gathers momentum and gusts along the front. Nightclubs in the daytime feel sad. Lonelier still, are these 'Gentlemen's clubs' – named without irony.

I cross the car park at the front and stand for a moment in what I'm sure must be roughly the spot where I stood just a few years back with Milky. We had been seeing each other for just a couple of months. I was twenty-four, but to me he was still the older boy at school. It was still a thrill. He was not only older than me, but in the year above my older sister who always was the distillation of cool, with half a can of mousse in her hair, lip-liner and a black Umbro jumper that I was desperate to have handed-down to me. When I finally did get it – it had faded to a disappointing shade of grey.

Milky and I buzzed though, with the electricity of our shared nostalgia that day in Yarmouth. But it had poured on us. I remember him shivering in just a shirt and a thin Harrington jacket, raindrops gathering on his glasses. Milky had a lot of stories of trips to town:

'We all went to the fair – two older lads shouted something as they walked out the pub we were passing. One of our lot decides to shout back at them and then run off. I was punched and headbutted while the rest watched from behind a fairground ride. Top mates!'

We had cut across the car park sharing a bag of sea-front doughnuts. They were delicious, but difficult to eat because of their tendency to be scalding hot but also unhelpfully delicate and tricky to handle. I remember I dropped about two thirds of mine onto the ground where we were walking. Not to be beaten, I quickly scooped it up and shoved it down the hatch. It tasted fine.

Milky said that he loved me – at that moment and in that spot. I remember looking at him and trying to smile, with the boiling hot doughnut burning inside my mouth. As we walked on, I felt the sprinkle of grit grinding between my teeth.

Aaron O'Farrell is a writer, filmmaker, and part-time actor from Dublin. In 2016, he won the UCD Maeve Binchy Travel Award for his documentary project *Looking for Sunday*, a film about a young Togolese man's struggles with homelessness and dreams of becoming a professional football player.

Togolese Gasoline

It was winter, but that doesn't mean much in West Africa. Lomé shimmered in the morning heat as Matt and I walked the streets searching for the cars that took passengers north out of the city. Clouds of cheap petrol fumes fogged the air as Chinese motorbikes and vehicles made of different coloured parts zigzagged in opposite directions. A chorus of tired horns battled with the Afro-Pop blaring from bars. Women called out to passers-by from stalls, offering discounts on mangoes and manioc that looked like driftwood. If ignored, they turned and complained to the women at their side who were deep-frying plantain beignets in vats of hot peanut oil. Children giggled and repeated the nursery rhyme they sang whenever they saw a white person.

'Yovo, yovo, bonsoir! Ça va bien? Merci.'

I nudged Matt and pointed to a group of men up ahead. They were leaning on old battered cars parked by the roadside, arms folded, indifferent to the chaos. They talked and smiled. In between jokes, their heads swept left and right, scanning for potential passengers.

We were spotted from a distance. Frenzied cries broke out as the men ran towards us, waving their arms. A crowd quickly formed, pulling at our shirts. Hands hovered before our faces brandishing an array of goods.

Pushing our way through, we glimpsed the vendors, hoping to avoid their eyes; women selling water sachets from dimpled steel basins atop their heads, children carrying loaves of yellow bread under their arms, young boys waving animal-hide jewellery; all barking prices.

The men pulled the merchants away, berated them, then formed their own crowd. Matt and I followed them to their cars wearing our backpacks on our front, hugging them close. Yelled commands echoed around us.

'Yovo, yovo! Ici! Avec-moi, yovo!'

'Kpalimé? Kpalimé? Vous allez à Kpalimé?'

'Les yovos, ici! S'il vous plaît!'

One of the men, the one shouting and pulling hardest, managed to rip my bag from me and walked with it towards his car. That meant we were going with him. Noticing this, the others slowly dispersed, mumbling their discontent. Some lingered to eavesdrop on the price I was going to pay, for future reference.

'Monsieur,' I called after our driver. 'Nous allons à Kpalimé.'

'Oui, Kpalimé.'

'Combien pour nous deux?'

He looked to the sky, hummed quietly, swayed his head, and then with a sympathetic smile gave me a price. I snorted a laugh in response, establishing negotiations.

'Je ne suis pas stupide, monsieur. Tu me-donnes le prix yovo, oui?'

He feigned offence at my accusation.

'Non, monsieur, c'est un bon prix.'

I offered a quarter of what he was asking. After much back and forth, him tutting in disbelief, we agreed on a fare that was one third of what I'd originally been quoted and more than what I'd been advised. The other drivers smirked.

Matt and I took our seats in the back, Matt sitting in the middle. A man in a suit carrying a briefcase sat beside him. A woman in a patterned dress sat in the front. We waited to depart as the original crowd of vendors flocked the vehicle, body-less arms dangling goods through the windows and sunroof.

Our driver rejoined the conversation outside. Long, slow minutes passed by as the sun baked the car. Matt and I felt suffocated from the heat and circulating dust. I could feel my T-Shirt dampening between my back and the seat.

I called out to our driver and asked when we would be leaving. When the car is full, came his response. I looked at the man in the suit, then nodded towards the woman in the front, and implied that the car was already full. The man in the suit and the woman laughed along with the drivers outside. Another two could easily be squeezed into the back, and absolutely in the front.

I turned to Matt and told him this. We didn't know each other well, having only met the week before in a bar. Both of us wanted to travel north on the weekend to see the waterfalls and jungle.

'What do you reckon?' I asked.

'Aw mate,' he sighed in his thick Australian accent.

I was relieved. 'What if we offer to just pay for two extra fares?' I said. 'Sure, it's only the price of a can of Coke back home.'

'Sounds good to me, do it,' Matt said, rearranging his tall legs into a more comfortable position.

I turned back towards the driver and made our offer. His friends listened in disbelief and shook their heads at us; crazy, pampered whites. Our driver got into his seat and started the engine. The car creaked onto the road, joining the traffic.

The man in the suit nodded at us, grateful for the extra space coming free of charge. In the front, the woman in the beautiful dress shuffled her knees, also savouring the legroom. Cold air began streaming through the rolled-down windows as we gathered speed, cooling the sweat on our heads. Lomé disappeared behind us.

Tall banana trees, corn stalks, and fields of dry green plants lined the road as we journeyed further north. The man in the suit opened his briefcase and took out a plastic soda bottle filled with salted peanuts. He tipped some into his palm, then passed the bottle around the car. The woman in front offered dry biscuits. Matt and I felt embarrassed for coming so unprepared.

'Merci, madame, monsieur.'

The car slowed as we approached a queue of vehicles inching through a toll booth. A man in uniform was greeting drivers while another made inspections, sometimes asking people to get out so he could check their vehicles.

Flooded rice paddies bordered both sides of the road. I leaned forward, head between my knees, and reached into my bag, rummaging for my camera to capture the landscape. Suddenly, I was thrown back as our car took off, racing past the queue and through the upturned barrier. The uniformed men shouted after us.

We all looked at the driver for an explanation.

'Calmez-vous. Ils sont mes amis,' he said, unconvincingly. He turned to the woman. 'Ils sont mes amis,' he repeated.

The old car began to rattle. Scenery passed by quicker than before. The air streaming through the windows pulsated with pressure, creating an unpleasant, vibrating clamour. A groan came from the engine as the car struggled with acceleration. I glanced at Matt. He looked uneasy.

'Qu'est-ce que tu fait!?' I demanded.

The driver didn't respond, his grip tightening on the steering wheel as the engine revved. The man in the suit also called for an explanation but got none. The driver checked his rear-view mirror, which framed his eyes. He was squinting, worrying.

The engine revved once more. We began swerving between oncoming traffic, forcing cars to veer away.

'Qu'est-ce que tu fait??!' I screamed along with the man and woman.

Our driver wouldn't answer, concentrating only on not hitting anything. He began driving on the wrong side of the road, overtaking other vehicles. As oncoming cars and motorbikes appeared, he weaved back across to the other side. Drivers beeped and screamed out their windows.

'Imbécile!'

My legs felt heavy, my stomach churned. Matt was shaking, burying his face in his T-shirt. I inspected the seat in front of me, wondering how it would take the impact of my body. Nobody was wearing a seatbelt; the car had none.

The man in the suit looked over his shoulder then began screaming at the rear window. I turned around and saw what he was screaming at. We were being chased by two cars – a saloon and a Chrysler Voyager minivan – as well as a policeman on a motorbike.

The saloon car caught up and drove alongside us. Driving, was another policeman. More men in uniform sat in the front and back, bellowing at our driver to pull over. Instead, he swerved left, aiming for them, attempting to ram them off the road. Both cars collided for a moment before the police car reduced its speed and fell behind, the metal of both vehicles screeching as they separated.

From the back seat, I began punching the driver in the arm, begging him to stop. The man in the suit did the same, both of us shouting. The woman in front made the sign of the cross with her hands.

'S'il vous plait!' We screamed.

The policeman on the motorbike pulled up beside us, waving an arm at the driver. Once again, our driver attempted to ram the vehicle, but the policeman pulled back in time. I offered our driver all the money I had on me to stop.

'Écoute le yovo!' screamed the man in the suit. 'Prend l'argent. Arreter!'

It was too late to offer money. Accepting meant stopping and being arrested. There seemed to be no way out for our driver as he swerved between cars, three police vehicles tailing us.

'Matt, we might have to jump.'

'No fucking way! We're going too fast.'

He was right. I could feel my insides tremble.

Up ahead, traffic had stopped and was spread across the road. A large tractor was attempting a three-point turn. Construction workers were ordering cars to halt and allow it to do so. They didn't see us approaching. This is it, I thought.

As the blockade grew nearer, I grasped the material of my shorts, bracing for impact. Then, our driver swerved right, and we began tearing along the dust path separating the road from adjacent fields. The construction workers saw us coming and dived out of our way. Having passed the parked vehicles successfully, our driver whipped the car sideways, back onto the road, now hoping to avoid a collision with the tractor. He was too slow.

The driver's side of the car collided with the tractor's tyre, ripping off the wing mirror, smashing part of the windscreen and putting a large dent in the rear passenger door. We came to a stop.

To my relief, having held onto Matt and braced myself for a shoulder barge with the seat in front, I was OK. Everyone was. It was over. But then, our driver accelerated once more, and the car moved away from the tractor.

However, the collision had damaged our vehicle so much we barely moved faster than ten kilometres an hour as the engine whined. Realising we couldn't get much further at this speed, our driver turned off the road and we rolled towards a cluster of houses. By now, we were going so slow I swung open my door and jumped out, stumbling onto my knees as the car came to a halt only a few metres away.

The driver burst his door open and fell out of the car, holding his arm in pain. With a limp, he ran towards the nearby fields, and was swallowed by the foliage.

—

'Please, you are OK?' said a man in fine clothes.

'Yes,' I replied.

'Come with me, I will take you to Kpalimé,' he said.

Matt and I followed him towards his car, the Chrysler Voyager minivan that had been tailing us throughout the chase.

'We will find him, very soon,' he said, assertively, though I didn't care. Matt and I were just happy to be out of a high-speed pursuit.

'Thank you, sir.'

'No, no,' said the man. 'After this? This situation was very serious. He is a very bad man, you know. Do you know why he was not stopping?'

'No.'

'He is a thief. In the car he was taking – *common on dit? Essence...* eh, gasoline?'

'We understand.'

'Beacoup, beaucoup gasoline! Very dangerous.'

Our driver had been using the guise of taxiing passengers as a means of smuggling large amounts of stolen petrol. I wondered what might have happened if we had hit the tractor full on.

Matt and I climbed into the back of the man's car. He sat in the passenger seat. A driver was already waiting, he shook our hands politely. The woman in the dress had disappeared. The man in the suit had followed the others into the bush in pursuit of our driver.

'Are you the police?' Matt asked.

'No, I am the chief – la maire de Lomé'

'Maire?' I probed. 'The mayor?'

'Oui.'

'Of Lomé?'

'Bien sûr.'

We sat in silence for a moment. The driver looked back at us through his rear-view mirror, noticed our confusion, and confirmed it, 'Oui, il est la maire.'

Matt and I exhaled faint laughter in disbelief and didn't ask any more questions. The car began moving.

Ivan Pope is an ideas-driven writer producing non-fiction and literary fiction using contemporary and historical events as starting points. He is also an artist who graduated from Goldsmiths Fine Art BA. Pope was an entrepreneur through the first days of the internet who published the first web magazine in the world and invented the cybercafé.

By Bicycle to Auschwitz

This is the point of remembering the Holocaust. It's not an act of honour for those who died, or an act of defiance against those who killed them. That's too easy. Rather, it is like the coin carried by an alcoholic, to remind him not to drink. To remember is to remain aware that we, as humans, balance on the very lip of the unspeakable; always far closer to toppling than we might wish to admit. All of us, everywhere, all the time.

—Hugo Rifkind, Holocaust Memorial Day 2015

The construction of my itinerary was swift and brutal. I decided upon a route: to follow the deportation trains from Paris to Poland. Taking an old map of Europe and a pair of dividers, I pressed the compass point into Oświęcim in modern-day Poland and stretched the jaws open until the pencil touched Paris. I rotated the arms, drawing a circle with a radius of one thousand two hundred and thirty-three kilometres. The perimeter of this circle embraced four million and seven hundred thousand square kilometres. I then inscribed a second circle, this time with a radius two hundred and sixty-five kilometres smaller than the first. These circles enclosed a doughnut-shaped circle of land and I call this a gyre, although technically it is an annulus, a ring with a hole in the centre. I continued creating these, one within another, until at the centre I have my destination.

Within the first gyre, moving clockwise from Paris, are Reims, Dunkirk, Amsterdam, The Hague, Antwerp, Gothenburg, Stockholm, Tartu, most of Estonia, half of Latvia, almost Tallinn and Helsinki, part of modern-day Russia, Pskov, Smolensk, Bryansk, Dnipro, the thousands of towns and villages where the Einstatzgruppen did their work, the Black Sea, Mykolaiv, Kherson, Sevastapol, a bit of Bulgaria, Istanbul, Thessaloniki, Corfu, Brindisi, Naples, Rome, Elba, Monaco, Marseille, Geneva, Lyon, Dijon and Paris.

The landscape carries a history of people, houses, fields, roadways, paths, fragments, remains, routes, signs, roads, railways, names, crossroads, waystations, museums, memorials, encampments, death sites, prisons, burial sites and graves, all of which I will pass on my way to the centre. To take in swathes of landscape, geography and history, I construct these gyres which sweep in huge circles around the disappearing point. I set out to cross this landscape, the well-worn paths, the glib generalisations, the denial, the acceptance, the memorials, the past used to shore up the present.

Cyclists have a cadence at which they feel most comfortable, chosen to minimise muscular fatigue, not metabolic demand. Any particular cyclist has only a narrow range of preferred cadences, the idea being to keep pedalling at the same rate at all times to achieve varying speeds. Treading water and doing doggy paddle is a cadence. The rate at which the feet move in the water is the rate of movement that will keep you afloat and alive. Cadence is what keeps us upright and alive in life. Lose your cadence and you are on a downward spiral to death. The rhythms with which we eat and shit, meet friends, laugh and cry, wake and sleep, that is our cadence. Without cadence, decadence.

When war came to Europe, the Jewish population adapted their cadence in response to external events, which varied from place to place, from community to community, from person to person and from camp to camp. The aim was to apply the rate that would keep you alive without hastening death. Even on the trains, even in Auschwitz, on the threshold of death, there was a cadence, finely judged and ultimately futile.

By chance, I heard Radio 4's *Book at Bedtime*, from Primo Levi's *The Periodic Table*, the life of a carbon atom. It was, Levi says in the text, his 'first literary dream... insistently dreamed in an hour and a place where my life was not worth much''. Levi's atom is liberated by a pickaxe ('all honour to the pickaxe and its modern equivalents') and falls into a lime kiln where it is roasted and separated from the calcium. Issued from the chimney, it is lifted ten kilometres high and breathed in by a falcon. It is dissolved three times in the water of the sea and travels with the wind for eight years, eventually entering a leaf, where it is separated from its oxygen. Combined with hydrogen and phosphorus, it forms part of a molecule of glucose, travels into a grape, is made into wine, gets drunk, resides in the drinker's liver for a week and then, when needed in response to sudden exertion on the part of the new owner, it becomes glucose again. The carbon is dragged in the bloodstream to the thighs, where it is brutally split into molecules of lactic acid, 'the grim harbinger of fatigue'. This is what I feel when I cycle up a hill. Levi will be with me all the way.

1 Primo Levi, The Periodic Table, 1975

I like the bite of the chain on crank at the top of a hill. After a struggle against your body, against your mind, legs burning, lungs pumping, there's suddenly a moment of release as gravity looses you from her challenge and sets you free for a moment. You can't really anticipate on a hill where this will occur. Looking up ahead to see where the hill crests, flattens, gives up, doesn't really give you much idea of when you'll get that pleasure. But you know it's there. Push, push, push and suddenly an unlatching comes, the need to change down from the insanely hard gear you've been struggling with, there, just there, comes the feeling of chain bite against cog. Now pushing against the pedal is rewarding again, pleasure, payment without pain. The hill has been beaten, the crest is with us, then the downhill. Then another hill. I like hills, they reward me. I can cover a mile in between two and eight minutes, depending on whether I am going up or down hill. Mostly it's about four minutes or fifteen miles an hour. It will take me four thousand minutes to cover my one thousand miles.

In Paris I cycled in hot sunshine from the Gare du Nord to Drancy transit camp in Eastern Paris. The Germans and the Jews, the collaborators and the bureaucrats, the guards and the policemen are long gone. These buildings could be any modern block of flats in any suburb of any city in the Western world, except that on the open side of the square is a railway wagon, a deathless cattle truck, installed on a tiny piece of track, as a memorial. There is a small hedge around the site and someone has taken advantage of this cover to take a shit next to the carriage. It is a sister railway wagon to others. I saw my first, years before, in the Washington Holocaust Museum. There are many more around the world now. I wonder where they have been all the years when nobody cared what they had been used for.

In nineteen forty when Paris fell, the German authorities seized an unfinished development whose high-rise towers were among the first of their kind in France, and converted it into a police barracks. La Muette, the Silent City, had been started in 1931 by Henri Sellier, the director responsible for social housing in the Paris region. He approached the architects Marcel Lods and Eugène Beaudouin with a plan to build a modernist urban community incorporating the first American-style skyscrapers in France. La Muette was everything that modernism aspired to be: sleek, sophisticated, technically challenging. In 1941, under the command of the Gestapo Office of Jewish Affairs in France and German SS Captain Theodor Dannecker, La Muette became an internment camp and took a new name from the neighbourhood in which it stood: Drancy. On August 20th, 1941, more than four thousand Jews were arrested and interned. The airy open spaces of its courtyards were enclosed with barbed wire and guarded by French gendarmes. A further round-up brought more than thirteen thousand more Jews to Drancy. By August the following year the transports had begun. Almost five thousand prisoners were swiftly despatched by train to Auschwitz.

I was eager to get on the road, out of the city, along the Marne, towards the East. I didn't want to waste time hanging out with shops and pavements. My bike was heavy with the equipment for the long journey and, not being used to it or to this traffic, I wobbled around each corner slowly, not sure how to turn without dipping sideways. I carried panniers front and aft, a handlebar bag, a tent strapped on the back, everything I needed for a journey across three countries was on the bike. I'm riding a vehicle made from skinny steel and rubber, powering it with my legs which have to pump up and down, up and down for every inch of the route. I was fit, but not too fit. Everyone had told me that the first few days would be the worst, that they would hurt, but after that I should become a lean pedalling machine. I didn't look forward to those first days, but I wanted to be that cyclist. The journey I had planned was long enough to allow for things to happen. The destination was always in sight, it resided within me. I was in modern Europe, hoping that I could throw myself back seventy years.

I carried maps, in digital form. This meant that I knew where I was going, but never where I was. It's a modern form of travel which echoes older methods. Always adrift at a precise location in the landscape, out of the city, the Seine marked the start of a ribbon across the continent. The route is one thousand miles from end to end: Bobingy, Epernay, Chalons sur Marne, Revigny, Bar le Duc, Lerouville, Novéant sur Moselle, Carling, across the German border to Saarbrücken, Frankfurt am Main, Dresden, on into Poland and Nysa, Katowice, then Auschwitz-Birkenau.

I left Paris along the Seine, my bike an old but beautiful tourer with four panniers. I carried a cooker so I could stop anywhere. The sun shone. I headed east. Although I knew my destination, each part of the route was a mystery. The railway lines crossed and recrossed my path, the same tracks, I think, which, a thousand miles down the road, would reconnect at Auschwitz. I stopped by a river and brewed some coffee. I'm all alone. Nobody knew where I was. I liked that.

I had a thought: was I following the railway, or was the railway following me?

When I got deep into the countryside I felt fear and sadness. I knew this journey wasn't about either, but leaving anywhere can be frightening and unnerving. Leaving a city to cross the huge empty spaces with only the fragile frame of a bicycle was unsettling. I'd hitch-hiked across Europe before, when I was young with nothing to lose, but where I'm headed now suddenly seemed impossible. Could such a place exist in the same world as me? Maybe, in relation to every village, town, city, street, road, house, shop, high street, to what we know, my destination is impossible. I still had to climb through Germany and crest the Czech Republic before starting my descent towards the remnants of hell. I couldn't feel the grey from where I was.

When my son was tiny I would fly on business around the world and sometimes, on an aeroplane in the middle of an endless night, I would find myself weeping silently in the dark. After one long trip when I got home my son refused to talk to me and I gave up my business life soon after. I sold the company and though I was wealthy for a short time, then ruined, I kept close to my children, which was what really mattered.

Saloni Prasad brings an uncommon mixture of science and humanities in her writing. She is currently working on a memoir packed with witty and dark humour, chronicling the journey of a young woman – herself, searching for her identity, as an antidote for meaninglessness in the aftermath of her father's death.

A Tale About Awful Dancers

I was six and she was four. It was hate at first sight.

I remember I was cute, as kids are during that age, even though I was just a skeleton covered in skin, sporting a dusky complexion, a smile with a prominent tooth gap and hair styled as an inverted bowl which somehow suited me. Undeniably, she was cuter with fairer skin and a chubbier face framed perfectly by her lustrous bob cut hair. I had met her at my dance classes where I was learning an Indian classical dance form called Kathak. She was the daughter of my dance teacher. Though not officially a student herself, many times she would dance along with us. She didn't know the alphabet beyond A, B, C, D but she knew every step to every beat. Her body swirled hypnotically. Her arms and her tiny ankles, accessorised with a string of small bells called Ghungroo, moved along in perfect harmony. She was undoubtedly a delight to watch.

Her arrogance made sense to me. Certainly, if I had been as gifted as she was, I would have been a bit proud myself. But that doesn't really explain the way she treated me. Usually, she would refuse to acknowledge my existence altogether. On other days, she would start yowling the moment I would try to talk to her. And once, she decided to take a step ahead and struck her Ghungroo on my face. The scar still persists on my forehead and more so in my memories.

Maybe I am being unfair. Maybe I did, in some way, have something that invoked irritation but, damn it, I wish I could have reciprocated with equal hatred. I tried to channel my inner Gandhi. I tried being friendly despite my earlier failed attempts in doing so but I ended up adding one more failure to the list. Nevertheless, I do believe that she has been a special person in my life, because no one has ever loathed me the way she did.

Dancing was easy when I didn't know how to do it. When I started training, I realised how horrible I was at it. My dance teacher didn't like me. She asked me to practise harder. I never did. The more I sucked at it and the more important it became for me to practise, the less motivated I grew. The lack of synchronisation between my mind and my limbs wasn't just limited to dancing. It later metastasised into sports as well – of all kinds. Being tall and skinny as a teenager, I was always asked to be part of the basketball team, that is, until they watched me play. I tried my hand at cricket, football, volleyball, table tennis, and badminton; the conclusion was always the same – I was horrendous. I also tried running, but despite my long legs I was slow. Kabaddi, another popular sport in India which is a mixture of wrestling and rugby, was clearly out of my league right from the beginning. My acute lack of talent didn't hinder me from participating though. I knew I could never be a national player or anything, but I could still play for the sake of it. Little did I know how terrified my friends were of me because of my terrible skills. They avoided playing with or against me fearing their own skills might deteriorate in my company. I was always picked last in every team and every time that happened, I was exposed to the horrified expressions of my friends.

I yearned to excel at everything. When I failed to achieve that, my incompetency tormented me. Impressing people, especially my parents, was essential to me. To save myself from the embarrassment of my obvious ineptitude, I started avoiding sports. I stayed in the classroom and doodled in my sketchbook instead. I found a sympathetic friend in those sketches. I found solace in books, but there too I was ridiculed for being a nerd. However, when I wasn't immersed in books I was accused of not studying enough. I was expected to read, read a lot, not the novels or short stories which were what I usually preferred, but academic books in order to have a spotless scholastic record. In retrospect, it seems I was shockingly tolerant of this absurd criticism in my childhood and during my teenage years. No comment, no action ever drove me to rage. I silently agreed, wept at night, and went on with my life caring just enough to be hurt but not to do anything about it. My art teacher loved me though. I don't paint anymore but I remember being decent at it. When I made a farewell greeting card for her, she flaunted it to everyone she knew. This appreciation was a refreshing change. But sadly, that didn't amend anything. By the time I finished my schooling, despite getting excellent grades in most of the subjects, I was rendered absolutely devoid of self-esteem. My heart didn't care for things that I could actually be good at. It longed for those that I wasn't meant to pursue.

My dance teacher often cited my example for how one shouldn't dance. But my mother, convinced that I could still learn and eventually be better at this art, wouldn't let me quit. Sucking at dance was deeply distressing because I genuinely used to enjoy it until it became a structured, formalised, theorised thing to learn rather than a random, fun and free form of expression. Of course, my reluctance to put in more sincere efforts can be blamed for my ineptness but no other student ever practised either. They exclusively danced during the classes and still they aced. I tried doing the same, but I failed. I guess that is where natural talent enters, something which I desperately tried to believe I still had in me.

But I didn't. I think that's the reason why 'the talented daughter' of my dance teacher was averse to me. Despite being so terribly young, she was a beautiful dancer. I guess I hated her for being so good. And she hated me back for being equally bad. That's how the waltz between my inferiority and her superiority complex went on until I finally quit the classes after four traumatising years.

Before my classes came to an end, I remember once it seemed to me that things might change after all. Throughout the class, I had taken special care of my hand gestures. I didn't stop smiling, just as an ideal dancer wouldn't, even though my cheeks hurt. I was conscious of my eye and neck movements. I had tried hard using my feet in sync with my arms and hands. I had tried being as graceful and as expressive as I could be. I spotted my dance teacher smiling at me and I couldn't help but wonder that I might have finally succeeded in dancing well.

She called me after the class. For the first time in my life, I was about to receive a compliment from her. I had finally done it. I had finally impressed her. Maybe she would start liking me now. Maybe her daughter would start liking me as well. I approached her brimming with happiness. Was she finally going to say the three golden words – 'You were good'? 'I heard you stood first in the drawing competition,' she said. I nodded. It wasn't something I expected to hear but the conversation had only begun, and it wasn't a bad beginning. The best was yet to come. And so, it came.

'You should draw, not dance.'

Michigan-born Kate moved to Northampton with her mum at the age of three. After completing a foundation diploma in Art and Design, she gained a first class degree in history and politics from UEA. She is also the editor of UEA's student arts magazine *Venue*, where her writing is regularly published.

White Out

I am sitting in a café opposite a man I do not know. The tables around us are occupied with people working, chatting, eating. They are all bundled up, to varying degrees; some have removed their scarves but not their coats, others have removed their coats but not their hats.

The man at my table has kept his coat on. It is made of black wool. He has dark hair and rectangular glasses with thick black frames. I'm not sure how old he is but right now I am scanning my eyes over the grooves and lines of his face as subtly as I can, peering up from over my laptop, and I estimate his age to be around forty-five; probably too old for me. His ears stick out from the side of his face like satellite dishes from a space station.

My fingers hesitated over the keys of my laptop before committing that unflattering description to the screen in front of me, lest he looks over my shoulder and sees it.

On his approach to my table, he said, 'excuse me, do you mind if I sit here?'

To which I responded: 'Oh, no! Absolutely. Go ahead. Let me move my stuff.'

'I haven't seen it so busy in here for a long time,' he commented.

I agreed: 'I know, me neither.'

'I suppose it's because everyone is working here, instead of uni.'

I smiled and slid my laptop and glasses case away from his side of the table, making room for him.

'Oh, it's OK!' He said merrily. 'My laptop isn't as big as yours.'

I smile. Great. He sits down. Pulls out his laptop. I go back to my writing.

Monday morning brought with it the first signs of snow. Thick flakes fell around me as I walked with my friends to the coffee shop where we had agreed to meet for lunch. Snow fell into my eyes, settled around my chin, in the pouch of my scarf. It was the first time in months we had all been together – having gone our separate ways since finishing our undergraduate degrees – and there was much catching up to be done. I had recently ended my relationship of three and a half years, and another friend had become engaged to his girlfriend. We asked him if it was hard organising a wedding (yes); was he scared (no); were they thinking of having children soon (no).

'I've never really imagined my wedding,' I lied. 'The only thing I'm sure I want to do in my life is be a mum.'

We discussed hypothetical weddings and hypothetical baby names, though for some the conversation was more hypothetical than for others.

Yesterday, I opened my blinds and saw white. I mean that in the most literal sense; I do not mean that I could see layers of beautiful white snow adorning the familiar scene outside of my window, but that the familiar scene had vanished completely.

I pushed the window upwards and open (my room is located in the attic, and the windows slope in accordance with the roof) in order to assess the situation further. The wooden frame around the glass seemed to crunch as the snow around it dislodged. Snow fell into the room, down the gaping sleeves of my dressing gown, onto rumpled bedsheets.

'Shit,' I said, before closing the window again.

I ate my breakfast alone in the living room whilst scrolling through my emails. Thursday's seminar was cancelled; the guest seminars I was scheduled to attend were cancelled; my fitness class was cancelled; though I have yet to hear for definite, the friend who is meant to be visiting me this weekend from London has likely, also cancelled. My life, for the foreseeable future, seems to be cancelled.

Tired of staring at four white walls and three white windows, I accompanied a friend – whose seminar was not cancelled – onto campus. 'I have nothing to do today,' I told him.

'It's brave of you to be walking onto campus today then, with this weather,' he said.

'No,' I reiterated, because he didn't seem to understand. 'I have *nothing* to do today.'

He laughed and I laughed, but there was a fear inside me beginning to grow.

The man stands up from our table and walks away, and I take the opportunity to survey the things he has left in his wake: a laptop; a pen; a brown leather notebook, cracked with age. I take comfort in the clutter belonging to another person, the paradoxical combination of homeliness and intrigue it ascribes to its curator. I am tired of the objects that orbit me: a scratched brown glasses case indented with the words *London Retro* in bold typeface; a black phone that illuminates with a painted giraffe on a bright turquoise background whenever I check the time; a slightly warped plastic water bottle with a tattered blue label. Privately I hope this collection inspires curiosity in others, but for me, it is devoid of mystery, compiled from objects of disinterest.

I imagine the man coming back to our table.

What's in your notebook? I would like to ask. *And why is it so cracked?*

It's the notes of a horrific murder case I'm currently investigating, he might say. *It's cracked because I've been a murder detective for twenty years, and I take this notebook everywhere I go. I get a huge sense of satisfaction out of helping the community, and I always like to be ready with my notes, if I'm needed. You would be surprised how frequently I am called upon, how often my talents and skills contribute toward the betterment of society.*

Or maybe: *It's a novel I'm working on. Set in the Cold War. It's cracked because I've been working on it, slaving hopelessly away at it, for the past twenty years. I'm always adding to it and editing it, but I'm never satisfied. I doubt that I will ever finish it, let alone publish it. I carry it with me everywhere I go, in the hope that inspiration will strike. But really, it just acts as a reminder of the things I could have achieved, if my life had turned out differently.*

I imagine him looking at my belongings and asking: *and you, what are you writing about on your laptop? And is that giraffe screensaver on your phone a photograph of something you painted yourself?*

I remember, seven weeks earlier, explaining to my housemate that I was likely going to end my relationship; trying to put into words for her (and myself) the pros and cons of doing so. She was preparing her dinner in our small kitchen, and I was sitting on our faded sofa, picking at the sleeves of my jumper.

'I think what helped me the most when I broke up with my boyfriend,' she said, as she shuffled through her pots and pans, 'was just keeping busy.'

Her words were comforting. She too had suffered, and yet here she was: her hair was washed, her face was clean, and the jar of pasta sauce in her hand evidence she was feeding herself. Her life had continued on. But once, she had been as I was then: indecisive and self-pitying, cut-free and floating. I felt the opportunity for a connection. I wanted to explain to her, for her to understand, the complexities and nuances of the way I was feeling. To lay bare for her, in some sort of logical order, the jumble of thoughts jostling for precedence in my head.

'It's just...' How to articulate the way I feel? '....so shit,' I said, and began to cry; the most basic of bodily reactions communicating to her my feelings where words had failed.

She popped her head around into the living room and offered a warm, sad smile. I could see her wondering whether to hug me, but she didn't. I think I am a rigid person. I am not cold but I have the air of someone who is, logistically speaking, hard to hug.

Instead, she offered more words. She told me of a friend who had found herself in a similar situation to mine, had been with her boyfriend for several years. They got on well, enjoyed each other's company. Yet, this friend of my housemate continued to be troubled by a persistent, unwelcome feeling she could never quite articulate; the feeling that something was amiss, that something was deeply wrong, that something just... wasn't quite right.

I asked my housemate how her friend resolved the problem, and she told me she had chosen to end the relationship. I nodded sadly. The story resonated with me. This girl I did not know had made the right decision ending her relationship, I thought, and because of this stranger's experience and my reaction to it, I realised that I too, would have to end mine.

'Yeah. That makes sense,' I said. And then asked, just to make sure, 'was your friend all right, in the end?'

'Yeah, she was.' My housemate reassured me. 'They were both miserable for like, eight months, but she's so much happier now.'

This morning, as I put on my mascara, in morning light dulled by a layer of snow, I thought: only six months of misery to go.

I have been writing for an hour, absorbed fully by the task. Now, I find myself slipping out of my head, back into the coffee shop. I notice, once again, the man sitting across from me, and consider sharing with him some of what I have thought and experienced in the last hour. Perhaps I could be light and jovial. We had, after all, enjoyed a brief introduction when he first sat down in front of me. I could say something like:

My writing is going quite well today! Sometimes it's a bit of a slog, but today I feel as if I am on a roll. What am I writing about? It's sort of about being in your early twenties, and feeling a bit scared.

But why should I say that, when the thing I would like to say most, is:

I have noticed that a lot of great writers are troubled; great, but solitary and damaged. I would like to be a good writer, but I don't want to be haunted, or broken.

This week, I have read two books by Jeanette Winterson, and it breaks my heart and terrifies me that there are children all over the world who grow up unloved and unwanted. Does that sound stupid? I guess it shouldn't be a revelation. I suppose it's something I've always known, but never really realised. I think there's a difference between knowing something and realising it, don't you?

The more I read, the more I realise how much there is to be afraid of, and how little the world owes us. So far I have been lucky; I have not known what it means to be truly alone. But do you not think that eventually my luck will run out? Why should I be allowed to go through life happy, loved, and healthy, when so many others are not?

Tell me, when you were twenty-three, did the world seem like a terrifying place to you? And now that you're older, has it all been as bad as you feared it might be?

A while later: The man begins to make movements as though he is leaving. Scarf wraps around his neck, laptop slides into its pouch, hands fumble into a pair of industrial looking gloves. His expression alters slightly with each task.

'Thanks for letting me share your table!' he says, kindly.

'You're welcome!' I respond as I turn slightly, almost calling out to him as he passes me.

After he has gone, I turn and look back towards the glass door he has exited from.

Outside, the snow continues to fall.

Sureshkumar Pasupula Sekar is a mechanical engineer by education, a software programmer by profession, a music aficionado and a writer by passion. At the University of East Anglia, studying MA in Biography and Creative Non-Fiction, he has been attempting to coalesce the musicologist with the memoirist in him. He recently secured a place on a PhD programme at the Royal College of Music, London.

I'm the King of the World

Twenty minutes into the film *Titanic*, when Rose (Kate Winslet) begins to recount the story, the camera slowly pans away from her close-up to the flickering screens behind. We see video footage of the corroded remnants of the sunken ship. The flashback begins. The debris gradually peels off its rust and scar to regain the glossy skin that *still smelled of fresh paint* once.

Matching the spatial and temporal contours of the moving images is the musical score. The snare roll is marching on. The strings section is ascending and gathering momentum in a tempo dictated by that of the seamless transformation of the remnants into reminiscences. Precisely when the transition from the present to the past is complete, like the fizz rushing out of an uncorked bottle of soda, the orchestra pops open with a loud crash of cymbals. Fleeing berserk on strings like an enslaved bird freed from its cage is the motivic melody that embodies the beauty and might of the ship Titanic. That crashing sound of cymbal hit me like a bolt of lightning. I became a fan of the symphonic film music at once.

Jurassic Park was the only Hollywood film I had seen before *Titanic*. I hadn't yet the ear and acuity to differentiate John Williams's rapturous score from T Rex's thunderous roar. There, however, were indelible scores composed by Maestro Ilaiyaraaja for Tamil films I grew up watching in the '90s in India. During my childhood, I must have been involuntarily developing a sensibility for music applied to the motion picture through Ilaiyaraaja's permeating scores.

The portal to the world of film scores had already been unlocked but left ajar. It was James Horner's score in *Titanic* that swung the door wide open.

I was fourteen. I hadn't any idea of the significance of precision in a musical score required to make it tightly synchronous with the visuals in a film. Leitmotifs, incidental music, contrapuntal music – I hadn't heard these terms. I didn't know that in *Titanic's* score, synthesised sounds and voices were interlaced with orchestral music to create a unique soundscape. I didn't have to know. The *Titanic* score was simple, earnest and its effect direct.

I was enthused. I would do everything I could to listen to more symphonic music. I was on an indefatigable quest to possess the *Titanic* score with decent audio fidelity on a cassette.

I found, at a friend's place in Salem, a *Back to Titanic* cassette with Jack (Leonardo Di Caprio) and Rose's *I'm Flying* pose on its deep oceanic blue front cover. I must have heard the score once while I was there for a group study session with the other classmates. That wasn't enough, and the place wasn't right. It was difficult to immerse into music amidst the chitter-chatter. I couldn't borrow the cassette and I didn't think I could buy it because I presumed it unavailable in Salem. I also noticed the price on the cassette cover; I quashed the thought of owning it.

I heard the score again only when I watched the film on its Indian television premiere on New Year's Eve. I thought the end credits drew the curtains down with the Celine Dion song *My Heart Will Go On,* but there was more. I couldn't have possibly known this earlier. The operators never let the complete end credits play in any of the cinema theatres in India. They would abruptly switch the projection off within a few seconds, and the audience too would start to exit the hall immediately after the end.

The most exhilarating of all the cues in the score – *Take Her to Sea, Mr Murdoch,* I would gather later – played immediately after Celine Dion's love ballad in the end credits. It was already midnight. Everyone at home was asleep. I had to keep it low. I had to hug tight our 21-inch CRT TV with my left ear on the speakers to hear the score. Even though the sound was feeble, compressed, and monophonic, it was sublime.

The most vivid aural imprint in my memory of the *Titanic* score is the sound of the gently hammered orchestral chimes – a thinner church bell tolling sound. Orchestral chimes are used within the piece at the moments of transitioning from one section to another. Chimes have in their robust metallic clang a ring of divinity and otherworldliness that never fails to uplift me.

I was in tenth grade at the time, and I wouldn't hear the *Titanic* score again until after two years; when I would be in an engineering college, and when I could afford to buy cassettes. I was now what Rose's mother in *Titanic* might call with disdain, *new money.* My parents would offer me some pocket money, which I saved and splurged on music. I also owned a Philips two-in-one tape recorder; a gift from my parents for securing the first rank in class in the final board examination.

I was studying mechanical engineering in Trichy, where I found the biggest music shop I had seen so far. The *Rhythm Boss.* I could see the interiors of the shop through the glass door in the front. The shop had audio cassettes stacked like decorative tiles on all the three walls from floor to ceiling. The walls appeared mosaic painted with multiple hues of that of the cover art on the cassette boxes. The shop had an immense collection of music and a catalogue with the names of the movie soundtracks catalogued and sorted in alphabetical order and a detailed track listing. It was the first time I had the opportunity to dig Indian film soundtracks with instrumental music tracks. In the catalogue, I spotted two titles I didn't think I would find in their collection – *Titanic* and *Back to Titanic*. I made a mixtape with selected instrumental pieces listed as *Theme Music* from a wide range of Indian films, and I included a few tracks from *Titanic,* too. I knew most of the music cues in the *Titanic* score by heart, but I realised I didn't know their titles.

I picked the track titled *Southampton*. I remembered that in one of the shots at the beginning of the film a green luggage carrier pulled through the crowd of passengers waiting to board the ship; it had *Francis Ltd Southampton* written on it. I was convinced that the track *Southampton* must be the piece of music that plays when the Titanic departs from the port. Also chose the tracks *Rose* from *Titanic* and *An Irish party in the third class* from *Back to Titanic*.

The track *Rose* wasn't what I presumed it to be. The piece I craved for is in fact delivered under the title *Take her to sea, Mr Murdoch* in the soundtrack.

'Take her to sea, Mr Murdoch,' says the captain when he commands his associate Mr Murdoch to increase the speed of the ship. I didn't know that for a long time. I couldn't have discerned that the musical cue playing in Jack's *I'm-the-King-of-the-World* moment could be titled *Take her to Sea, Mr Murdoch*. When I watched the film the first time, I hardly understood the dialogue, for it was only the second English film I ever saw. Though English was our medium of education at school, the teachers who taught us in English didn't have the accents of characters in the film. And none of our schoolmates had with each other casual conversations in English.

It has been seventeen years since I first watched *Titanic* at the *Saraswathi* movie theatre in Salem. I am about to experience watching the film on a big screen again at the Royal Albert Hall. Conductor Ludwig Wicki with the Royal Philharmonic Concert Orchestra is performing the whole score live to the projection of the film. James Horner – the composer – and James Cameron – the filmmaker – are seated in the stalls. I am standing far from the stage up above in the general gallery.

The musicians in the orchestra aren't seated in a dark pit under the podium like they are in an opera or ballet performance; they are up on the stage and given the prominence of that of a lead singer in a band. Subdued golden yellow spotlights on sheet music stands illuminate the stage enough for the audience to observe the musicians, their musical instruments, and the conductor. The film projection screen is dangling high above the stage, behind the orchestra.

Titanic Live is a gala concert event meant for celebration, reverence, and indulgence in nostalgia. Many who are attending this event are here to celebrate a special occasion in their lives – birthdays, anniversaries, or a date night. Men are all suited up. Women glittered up. Couples hold each other's hands and peck on each other's cheeks. Outside, in the foyer, there is a mandatory souvenir stall selling the film merchandise – T-shirts, music CDs, the glossy programme book. And food. Popcorn. Ben & Jerry's. Crisps. Häagen-Dazs. Wine. Coffee. It is a quiet carnival.

We request the patrons to occupy their respective seats. The main event is about to begin. A booming voice alerts all the men hanging out at the bar and women waiting in a long queue outside the loo.

Lights are off. Coughs and claps subside. The screen wakes up. The conductor lifts the baton and waves at the orchestra. We slip into a collective dream.

A few minutes into the film, Jack is standing with his friend at the nose of the ship. So close to the edge that no part of the giant ship is in his line of sight. He is looking at the horizon. He is standing atop all earthly entities, like an emperor who just conquered the infinite ocean and summoned it to lay down at his feet.

When he begins to scream with unbridled joy, 'I'm the king of the world,' the camera's eye is looking at him from a distance, and from forty-five degrees to his right. The sunlight glistening on the surface of the ocean splashes over the sky in the background turning it into a glaring white. The movements are kinetic, dramatic and its effect is beguiling because everything is set in frantic motion. The ship is cruising forward, the camera is moving relentlessly in different directions; towards, away or sideways around the nose of the ship, with its eyes always fixed on Jack, who is in a state of nirvana.

The camera's movements are orchestrated like a symphony, with all the instruments at the director's disposal swivelling around a central motif that is Jack's infectious exuberance. James Horner's delirious score is applied to this sequence to unify and transform all the fervent visual acrobatics into one seamless moment of stillness.

Precisely when Jack screams 'I'm the king of the world,' with a loud thud of a percussion and the crash of cymbals, the 60-piece string section breaks free. I am standing still, clutching tight the handrails of the gallery. Strings soar high and above all the other orchestral layers, and at their peak pronounce the ship's theme aloud. At once, in an infinitesimal moment, the bombast of the score fires up an electric pulse through every cell in my body. A million things are set in motion. And voila! A small pearl of a tear in my eyes. Just a tiny moistening drop, forming a thin translucent film. The cruising images of the Titanic I behold in my eyes wobble as if they fell on the ripples in a pool of water.

Susan Woolliams enjoyed a variety of writing challenges before becoming a modern languages teacher. She has worked in London and internationally as a managing editor, translator, and freelance business writer. More recently, Susan's non-fiction writing has addressed a diverse range of themes including travel, sport, memory, education, and primate welfare.

The Paolozzis

Note: this is an imagined scene, based on *Eduardo and Emma Paolozzi: A Celebration of Art and Life,* an exhibition held during October 2015 at Paul Smith's flagship store in London.[1]

—

October, 2015

'Well *you* know what Dad was like – sort of magical, *always* collecting stuff … even old cigarette packets, anything that caught his eye. Just couldn't resist picking it up and pocketing it. S'ppose that's what a *great* artist *does*...'

By the time the train lurches out of Durham it's almost ten thirty at night. Coach E's only occupants are the owner of the confident, warm voice, and me, unable to doze off. The 'voice' is surely not aware of the insomniac eavesdropper seated a knight's move behind her on the King's Cross to Edinburgh express. As she yawns and leans forty-five degrees into the aisle to stretch her phone-free arm, I glimpse the sharp contours of her face and I assemble the visual clues: a full-figured mature woman in loosely fitting black silk; thick, dark curly hair swept back from a broad forehead and coiled into a relaxed chignon; a wide band of intricately-tooled silver adorning the left wrist of a plumpish, lightly-tanned arm.

'Yep, it's 9, Albemarle Street. Please come and see it – it's like going back fifteen years – wonderful memories.'

The urge to unpick the conversation is irresistible and two clicks on the iPad are enough to link my mystery co-passenger to an elegant address in Mayfair – the London flagship store of fashion designer Paul Smith.

'Honestly, the room's perfect – looks just like he's slipped out for tea. We've tried to recreate what I used to describe as a sort of... *harmonious chaos* from his studio days. You'll see magazines, lots of sketches, even half-finished artworks.'

I'm intrigued, Googling furiously for answers. Who *is* this woman? What's her link to Paul Smith? Who is the artist? And then follows the perfect sound bite:

1 www.telegraph.co.uk/art/artists/emma-paolozzi-working-alongside-her-artist-father-eduardo/

'OK well, for starters look at the Paul Smith website… then go to *Eduardo and Emma Paolozzi, A Celebration of Art and Life*. Bit of mouthful, yeah, but you know, it does what it says…'

Of course. I should have figured it out: Sir Eduardo Paolozzi, Scottish sculptor and surrealist artist born in Edinburgh to Italian parents, widely revered Pop Art pioneer (some say inventor) and inveterate collector, since childhood, of comics, toys, cigarette cards, and high street ephemera. I think of the iconic mosaics at the Tottenham Court Road Tube station, the hunched Newton sculpture outside the British Library; two of his multiple legacies to the British public. And I'm silent, awestruck, in the near company of his offspring.

Emma, I discover, is the youngest of Paolozzi's three daughters. There is enormous fondness in her voice when she speaks of her father, for whom she was the main carer during his post-stroke wheelchair-bound years until his death in 2005. Photos of them side by side reveal strikingly obvious physical parallels: Mediterranean looks, dark eyes under emphatic brows, generous lips and a sturdy physique. Emma has also inherited the Paolozzi artistic gene; with his guidance and collaboration, she's earned success as a jewellery designer. The 'Celebration' exhibition (directed by Emma and hosted at Paul Smith's Mayfair office) offers Paolozzi devotees a rare insight into his working life through a representation of his typically chaotic Chelsea studio.

I'm longing to break cover now. I want to know more. How did he really cope during the three months he spent in enemy alien internment during World War Two? And how did he overcome the tragedy of losing both his father and grandfather when the ship deporting them to Canada was torpedoed? But it's nearly midnight and I lack the courage to make an approach. So I listen, dry-mouthed but fascinated, as Emma Paolozzi responds to someone else's questions about her father:

'You should contact Terence Conran – Dad was his mentor, as well as a close friend… maybe you've heard the story about Dad teaching him to make black squid risotto?'

One of Terence Conran's most treasured possessions, recalls Emma, is a maquette of Paolozzi's Head of Invention sculpture in bronze, the original of which Conran commissioned to stand outside the first Design Museum at Butler's Wharf in London. For Conran, it seems, Eduardo Paolozzi had stood head and shoulders above the many other artists he admired.

Paolozzi's great friendship with writer J G Ballard is acknowledged and discussed. Ballard even claimed that, if by some calamity all art from the twentieth century were to be destroyed except for the work of a single artist, then it would be possible to recreate all of the century's greatest artistic developments if that artist were Eduardo Paolozzi.

'He was someone who liked to make use of everything, couldn't bear to throw things away. He told me years ago that sometimes he feels like a wizard in Toytown, transforming a bunch of carrots into pomegranates.'

As the train creeps into a hushed Waverley Station, I stand up to retrieve my bag from the overhead shelf and I catch sight of her salvaging an elaborate purple and gold foil wrapper from the seat in front of me. She half smiles at me and pockets the wrapper. Sort of magical.

Sister Christa

It's just past midday on a scorching Monday in late June. I stray from the woven redbrick path and step over a fringe of long grasses onto sweet-smelling summer turf. I have to make my way lightly, tiptoeing between headstones, to avoid the heels of my slingbacks sinking into patches of spongy moss. The only sounds come from above, echoing childhood summers spent nearby: the soft call of a collared dove sheltering in the canopy of a birch, and the distant rumble of a passenger jet, trailing gauzy white across a perfect, cerulean sky.

Pointing heavenwards to my left is the church's slate-grey steeple. It sits, oddly conical like a witch's hat, on top of a square, buttressed tower. There's a decorative black weather vane at its summit, and on the south side of the tower the sun's rays highlight golden Roman numerals against a matt black clock face.

The fifteenth-century sandstone walls of St Peter & St Paul's propose cool sanctuary from the afternoon's heat, but I'm pressed for time, already scanning names and dates on the jumble of leaning headstones and monuments surrounding me. The departed who lie hereabouts pre-date my ex-headmistress by at least two hundred years. I know from my research that her journey ended here. But where exactly is her grave?

There's nobody else about, apart from the doves overhead and the old souls beneath my feet. Perhaps I should abandon my search. Is it a bit ghoulish to look for the grave of an ex-teacher?

In a final, haphazard bid to identify Sister Christa's last resting place, I rejoin the path to skirt the church's perimeter. My heels are now ringing impatiently against the brickwork and I pause intermittently to frown over barely visible, timeworn inscriptions. I look skywards in hope of a divine revelation.

My prayer is rewarded within about thirty seconds. I just happen to glance over a low stone boundary wall, towards the other side of the lane, and I spot a regiment of neatly-tiered stone memorials, standing proud beyond a black wrought-iron fence. Here, an overflow graveyard plot slopes downhill to reveal row upon soldierly row of contemporary-style headstones. The dates should be legible, I think, but I wonder if the graves are arranged chronologically...

Even before I reach the churchyard's little wooden gate to cross the road, I notice a young, blonde woman peering at me from a half-open side door of the church. She steps out, in full clerical dress, to offer assistance and a further revelation.

'Aha. You mean the nuns' plot? Yes, I'm pretty sure they're all together down there at the far end, to the right of the pathway, near the boundary hedge.'

I had assumed that a Catholic nun in Anglican territory would be here alone, an anomaly. I ask myself who else from my schooldays could be buried here. Calmer now, and curious, I stride downhill and come upon the grouped headstones of my former headmistress, four of her 'sisters', and Mr Arthur Walker, the school's first caretaker.

In the furthest, shadiest corner of the graveyard, where the air smells loamy and the dark green glossy shrubs are intertwined with ivy, I see *her* name first in the line of half a dozen identical memorials. The slim, grey marble slab sits as though only recently risen from the potpourri of desiccated leaves and stray twigs at its base. Its plain, knee-high rectangular form is softened by the gentle curve of its top edge, drawing the eye to a simple Christian cross, engraved in a plain serif font above the inscription.

✝

OUR BELOVED SISTER
M CHRISTA SCHMITT SSND[2]

4. NOV. 1915 – 9. OCT. 1984

R I P

I've known for the past week that she died in 1984 – only seven years after I left school – but this stark authentication of her relatively early passing triggers an unanticipated wave of sadness, followed in equal measure by ripples of contrition and self-doubt I sometimes experienced in her presence at school.

In those days, rather like a Chief Dalek, Sister Christa would glide noiselessly along the main school corridor, to appear in a classroom doorway with tightly-clasped hands and glaring disapproval written into pale, fierce eyes. Frequently, her disapproval resulted from an appearance-related offence; to be caught with over-plucked eyebrows or bare knees showing just below the hitched-up hemline of one's ugly brown school kilt would result in immediate censure.

In her prime, Sister Christa had represented a wholly dominant and

---

2 School Sisters of Notre Dame

seemingly unassailable force at the school. At times, her no-nonsense brand of discipline, delivered in grammatically-perfect, German-accented English, even inspired fear. It also inspired a truly abhorrent nickname – 'Hitler' – and naive but appalling acts of caricature: students goose-marching silently behind her, aping the Nazi salute. I am ashamed now at how unappreciative we were of her considerable qualities as an educator and a leader; how ignorant we remained of her sacrifices and her determination to provide those in her care with a stable, moral foundation for life. I wonder why she never recounted to us the story of her escape from Nazi Germany to England, as a young novice, and her subsequent arrest and internment on the Isle of Man as an enemy alien. We had no idea of the great esteem in which she was held by the SSND, who elected her to Regional Leader for England. For us, she was simply an over-austere teacher-nun who, unaccountably and hilariously, wore a very obvious auburn wig beneath her wimple.

And here she lies, far away from her Heidelberg home, but in the fine and loving company of her religious family. No doubt I will never put to rest the ongoing speculation among my peers concerning the auburn wig, but I am grateful now for this occasion to pay long-overdue respect to a teacher I wish I'd known better.

Acknowledgements

Thanks are due to the School of Literature, Drama and Creative Writing at UEA in partnership with Egg Box Publishing for making the UEA MA Creative Writing Anthologies possible.

Tiffany Atkinson, Trezza Azzopardi, Stephen Benson, Clare Connors, Andrew Cowan, Alison Donnell, Giles Foden, Sarah Gooderson, Rachel Hore, Kathryn Hughes, Thomas Karshan, Philip Langeskov, Timothy Lawrence-Cave, Jean McNeil, Paul Mills, Jeremy Noel-Tod, Denise Riley, Lisa Robertson, Sophie Robinson, Helen Smith, Rebecca Stott, Henry Sutton, George Szirtes, Matt Taunton, Ian Thomson, Steve Waters, Julia Webb, Naomi Wood.

Nathan Hamilton at UEA Publishing Project, and Emily Benton.

Editorial Committee:
  Justus Flair
  Faye Holder
  Laurence Hardy
  Yin F Lim
  Aaron O'Farrell
  Sureshkumar Pasupula Sekar
  Saloni Prasad
  George Utton

UEA Creative Writing MA Anthology: Non-fiction, 2018

First published by Egg Box Publishing, 2018
Part of UEA Publishing Project Ltd.

A CIP record for this book is available from the British Library.
Printed and bound in the UK by Imprint Digital.

Designed by Emily Benton.
emilybentonbookdesigner.co.uk

Proofread by Sarah Gooderson
Distributed by NBN International
10 Thornbury Road Plymouth
PL6 7PPT +44 (0)1752 2023102
e.cservs@nbninternational.com

ISBN: 978-1-911343-44-8